CONTENTS

The Costs of Constitutional Change

A Citizen's Guide to the Issues

George Fallis

James Lorimer & Company, Publishers
Toronto, 1992

Canadian Cataloguing in Publication Data

Fallis, George

1947-

   The Costs of Constitutional Change

Includes bibliographic references.
ISBN 1-55028-396-0 (pbk.)

1. Canada - Constitutional law - Amendments - Economic Aspects. 2. Federal-provincial fiscal relations - Canada.3. Quebec (Province) - History - Autonomy and independance movements - Economic aspects. 4. Federal government - Canada. 5. Canada - Constitutional law - Amendments. I. Title.

HC113.F34 1992   330.971'0647   C92-094658-5

Cover photo: Gary Castle

James Lorimer & Company, Publishers
Egerton Ryerson Memorial Building
35 Britain Street
Toronto, Ontario M5A 1R7

Printed and bound in Canada

Canada is on the verge of a major restructuring of the federation. At the same time, Canada's future economic prosperity and system of providing social programs are in doubt as never before. This book had its genesis in a belief that the economic implications of constitutional reform should be fully aired in the public debate. There has been an enormous amount of thinking and writing about the economics of federal states and Canada's constitutional alternatives. But it is mainly by economists directed at other economists. This book tries to make this material accessible to interested citizens to help them participate in constitutional redesign.

The Royal Commission on the Economic Union and Development Prospects for Canada (the Macdonald Commission) drew together hundreds of Canadian scholars in "the most extensive research program in Canadian history." Its output in the mid 1980s included a three-volume report and over 280 research studies published in seventy-two books. The Commission was to recommend "the appropriate institutional and constitutional arrangements to promote the liberty and well-being of individual Canadians and the maintenance of a strong competitive economy." It is not a gross simplification to say that the Macdonald Commission was a massive study of the economics of the Confederation debate.

Since the failure of the Meech Lake Accord, economists have worked further on constitutional issues. The John Deutsch Institute at Queen's University published two volumes of papers on *Economic Dimensions of Constitutional Change*. The 1991 Annual Review of the Economic Council of Canada was titled: *A Joint Venture: The Economics of Constitutional*

Options. The C.D. Howe Institute is publishing a series of economic studies, one group titled "Economics of Constitutional Renewal" and another group titled "Economics of the Breakup of Confederation." Additional background data and analysis are available from Department of Finance publications and those of the Canadian Tax Foundation. The bibliography lists all these papers.

That work forms the basis for this book . The debt is not just intellectual: analysis, examples and even language have been borrowed in writing this book. This is acknowledged here, rather than in each case, to escape an academic's often pedantic presentation.

The author also wishes to acknowledge other debts. The Walter and Duncan Gordon Charitable Foundation, the Canadian Imperial Bank of Commerce and the Bank of Nova Scotia generously supported the writing and distribution of this book. These financial supporters bear no responsibility for the ideas expressed herein. Several readers provided helpful comments. And most important, Peter Nicholson and François Vaillancourt stimulated and sustained my interest in the economics of the Confederation debate.

1

The Constitutional Dilemma

"Canada is grappling with twin crises — one of structure, the other more profound and delicate, of the spirit.

Both structure and spirit combine to make a blueprint for a society. But the spirit — that is, shared ideas, ideals, dreams and confidence — will in the long run overwhelm any structure, however ingenious.

The curse of our political system since the beginning has been to put structures first, last and always — then to wonder why nobody believed Canada was anything more than amending formulas, notwithstanding clauses and an awful lot of jurisdiction-crazy bureaucrats.

Now we face a spiritual crisis which demands we find, in a very short time, new structures we hope will last a very long time."

Keith Spicer, **Citizens' Forum on Canada's Future**

Constitutions are not simply abstract legal documents. Just as the rules define the game, so does the constitution — the fundamental principles of a nation that determine the powers and duties of government and guarantee certain rights to the citizens — define the country. Together these powers, duties and rights are the organic law of the land. The Canadian constitution — the *Constitution Acts, 1867 to 1982* — establishes a system of parliamentary government, provides a federal structure to that government by dividing the powers between national and provincial levels and contains the *Canadian Charter of Rights and Freedoms*. These frame our civil society.

What, you may ask, do the *Constitution Acts, 1867 to 1982* have to do with the price of beer or holding onto your job?

The answer is — plenty. It turns out that the division of powers under the *Constitution Acts* allows provincial laws that raise the price of beer in Canada while our unresolved constitutional tensions create economic uncertainty and divert attention from our pressing economic problems.

When we change the constitution, we change the society. Clearly we, the citizens, must participate in this new creation. We can't leave the discussions to the constitutional junkies — the lawyers, the politicians and the academics. Citizens must participate in creating a new constitution because it will express what it means to be Canadian. We must stay informed because constitutions have legitimacy *only* with the consent of the citizenry.

We must amend our constitution and renew our Confederation. Quebec has declared that Canada must offer substantial constitutional changes, or else a referendum on sovereignty will be held in October 1992.

Alternative Visions
Although Quebec has initiated the process, it is by no means the only participant. Most Canadians are familiar with the competing visions that must be accommodated in a renewed Confederation, and with their most obvious ramifications.

Quebec demands greater political autonomy to preserve and promote its collective identity and economic well-being. Constitutional recognition of Quebec's distinct nature would require greater powers for Quebec and the reform of national institutions. If Quebec alone among the provinces achieved greater powers, other provinces would oppose this asymmetry. But if all provinces were treated similarly, the country might balkanize.

Provinces outside of central Canada feel the federal government has not been sufficiently responsive to their aspirations and concerns. It has intruded in provincial affairs benefiting one region at the expense of another. These provinces want more representation at the centre, out of proportion to their population, through a Triple-E Senate: elected-effective-equal. But this would weaken Quebec and Ontario's relative power in national policy and undermine the basic democratic principle of representation by population.

Aboriginal peoples argue they have an inherent, historical right to sovereignty. They were self-governing before the arrival of European settlers; aboriginal self-government is not something to be granted by Canada, while negotiating about its precise meaning. They are inherently self-governing and will negotiate with Canada on the future form of existing sovereignties. While most Canadians are sympathetic to the aboriginal people, fewer would agree they have an inherent right to self-government. Some have concerns because the meaning of self-government is not yet established. To entrench an inherent right in a new constitution would hugely complicate matters for Quebec, if it ever chose to become a sovereign country.

A Pan-Canadian vision stands opposed to these regional and specific claims. It argues that provincial powers have become too great, fragmenting the economic union, eroding the sense of a national community and destroying the concept that Canadian citizens should be treated equally, wherever they live. A stronger central government is needed so Canadians can live and express themselves throughout the country.

The Charter of Rights and Freedoms is a defining feature of our nation for many Canadians. They want to remove the notwithstanding clause to make the Charter a powerful buttress for individual rights against government actions. Quebec will not accept the supremacy of individual rights in the Charter against the collective rights expressed by government action. Quebec's mission is to preserve the French-speaking collectivity, the island of six million French in a sea of 250 million English. Aboriginal peoples are also unlikely to accept the supremacy of the Charter.

These divergent political and philosophical views and the tensions between them have been widely discussed and are familiar to most Canadians. But there are economic issues as well. The costs of constitutional change must be addressed.

Economics and the Constitution

The opinions expressed by average citizens indicate that economics belongs on the constitutional agenda. The Citizens' Forum on Canada's Future heard the economy mentioned more than any issue except political leadership and participatory democracy. The economy was mentioned more than Quebec separation, language, cultural diversity or aboriginal problems.

Many Canadians feel pessimistic about the economy, especially because unemployment remains so high. However, we must separate the economic problems brought on by the current recession from the economic problems resulting from existing constitutional arrangements. The economic problems that legitimately belong in constitutional debates are long-run problems. They are problems that may require us to change the framework of how we approach them.

We should also remember that under our existing constitution, Canada's economy has performed well by international standards. The standard of living in Canada is the second highest in the world, only 5 percent below that in the United States, and we have closed the gap during the 1980s. Over the last thirty years, the real rate of economic growth in Canada has been higher than in any G-7 country except Japan, and higher than the Organization for Economic Cooperation and Development (OECD) average. The same is true even in the recent past. Economic success is not simply a

United Nations' Human Development Index		
Rank		
1970	1985	1990
Japan 9	1	1
CANADA 7	6	2
Iceland 3	2	3
Sweden 1	4	4
Switzerland 6	3	5
Norway 2	4	6
United States 12	10	7
Netherlands 3	7	8
Australia 11	8	9
France 8	9	10

Source: Dept of Finance, Quarterly Economic Review. June 1991

high per capita Gross Domestic Product (GDP). Surely it also means having an educated and healthy population. The United Nations has computed a Human Development Index — a summary measure of national income, literacy and longevity. In 1970 Canada ranked seventh among OECD countries, in 1985 it ranked sixth and in 1990 it ranked second. Only Japan ranked higher.

Despite our economic success over the last thirty years, the real worry is that there has been some fundamental change. Our prosperity may not continue for another thirty years because we have lost the formula for success.

Canada faces three great economic challenges. The first is fiscal — we must ensure that government deficits and debt are returned to manageable levels over the medium term. The second is to ensure our future prosperity in a globalizing and increasingly competitive world. The third is to sustain an economy and structure of government that can provide education, health care and income security for all Canadians. Meeting these challenges requires that the powers and duties of the federal and provincial governments be clearly established as well as the rights and responsibilities of citizens. In short, we must have an appropriate constitution. Our current attempts to deal with these economic problems have put great pressures on our federation.

Economic analysis is important in constitutional design because in a federal state the constitution establishes the framework for governments to carry out their economic responsibilities. How should powers be divided between federal and provincial governments? How should taxing powers be assigned? What sorts of transfers should flow between levels of government? What government structure is needed for fiscal policy, monetary policy and maintenance of the economic union? Economic principles can help in answering these questions of constitutional design.

The Fiscal Crisis

Between the early 1950s and the mid 1970s, the federal government managed its fiscal affairs well. In some years (indeed most years) the government ran a small deficit, but it also occasionally had a small surplus. Total public debt grew, but at a manageable rate. By the mid 1970s, the public debt was about 34 percent of GDP. This compares well with the period immediately after World War II when public debt was almost 150 percent larger than the economy.

Since the mid 1970s, however, the federal finances have deteriorated to the point of crisis. In 1974-75 the federal deficit was $2 billion. It rose in good years and bad over the next ten years until it reached $38 billion in 1984-85. The deficit has now stabilized at about $30 billion but public debt as a share of GDP continues to grow. Despite deficit stabilization, interest charges on the public debt have gone from 20 percent of federal expenditures in 1984-85 to almost 27 percent. Every recent federal budget has predicted the debt-to-GDP ratio would decline. It never has. Provincial-local debt ratios have doubled over the last decade. In the G-7 countries, only Italy has a higher ratio of total government debt-to-GDP.

Citizens are way out in front of politicians in recognizing the problem. They discussed the deficit far more frequently than any other economic issue mentioned at the Citizens' Forum on Canada's Future. A group discussion in Hay River,

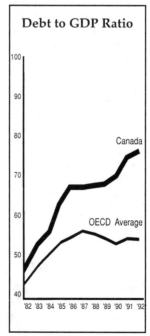

Source: OECD Outlook,
July 1991

Northwest Territories, told the Forum, "We are living beyond our means. Our inability to deal with our debt is the one thing that will destroy Canada."

The struggles to control the federal deficit and to stop the escalation of the public debt are affecting every aspect of public life. Premier McKenna of New Brunswick recently stated, "I say unequivocally that a major part of our current constitutional dilemma stems from our fiscal situation. The natural tensions which exist in Canada have been horrifically exacerbated by the constant grinding down of our fiscal capacity."

Cries for fiscal prudence too often include a neo-conservative agenda of reducing the role of government and cutting back on social protection. The two do not necessarily have to go hand in hand. Financial prudence and a strong public sector are not incompatible. The period to the mid 1970s proved this as total public sector spending in Canada grew from about 25 percent of GDP to 38 percent. Most of our highways, airports and transit systems were put in place. The Canadian welfare state was developed. Schools, universities and hospitals were built. National medicare was instituted. Unemployment insurance, old age pensions, welfare assistance and family allowances were paid and enriched. Yet, this was also an era of fiscal prudence.

The current fiscal crisis was not caused by a major expansion of the welfare state since the 1970s, indeed there have been few initiatives since that time. The blunt truth is that the programs we had in place became more expensive, and Canadians were unwilling to pay the taxes for them. Two additional complications worsened the situation. There was a major recession in the early 1980s with a slow, uneven recovery across the country. And real interest rates rose while real growth rates fell in the 1980s, with the result that paying interest on the public debt required increased taxes. Taxes did not go up enough.

Canada has special problems in raising taxes because the United States, our major trading partner and a place to which Canadian people and firms can easily move, has a relatively smaller public sector and therefore lower tax rates.

The public debt can only be brought under control by reducing deficits. While it is sometimes appropriate for a government to increase its deficit, for example during an economic downturn or to finance capital expenditures, neither of these can adequately justify the way fiscal affairs have been treated since the mid 1970s. If the government increases its debt during a downturn, it should also reduce it during the later stages of an expansion. Over the past twenty years the government exercised inadequate restraint during boom periods. Nor can the debt be explained as financing of capital investment.

Some of the debt did finance capital investment that is not properly recorded: by financing education and health care, debt is partly financing investment in human capital. Canadians will be better educated and healthier than they would have been, and therefore will earn higher incomes. But some education spending and much health spending is not investment. In any event these investments do not seem to have yielded a return sufficient to pay for themselves.

There is simply no escape from the fact that over the next few years Canadians must accept the dual medicine of expenditure restraint and tax increases. The only issue is the balance between the two. Provincial and local politicians want no part of what they see as Ottawa's problem. However, we pay taxes to all three levels of government and federal restraint will inevitably influence provincial and local finances. The federal fiscal crisis is not just a federal problem, it is a crisis for the nation and for all levels of government. It will be a problem for whichever party happens to be in power —Progressive Conservative, Liberal, New Democratic, Reform or Bloc Québécois.

Our Threatened Prosperity

In the mid 1980s, the Macdonald Commission wrote: "This Commission sees Canada as having attained a quite remarkable record of economic success. We believe, however, that the circumstances which brought about that success will not continue; indeed, they have already altered both globally and domestically. The differences which are emerging in our economic experience will have to be matched by differences in economic and social policies." This is even more true today as the pace of globalization and industrial restructuring has quickened. Our future prosperity is threatened.

In most industrialized countries, growth in real per capita

GDP has declined from the 1960s, to the 1970s, to the 1980s. Canada's growth rates have also declined from the 1970s to the 1980s, and in the last decade we had a per capita growth rate below the OECD average. Despite the slower growth, the public sector kept growing, taking an ever-larger share of the economy. In recent years, there have had to be tax increases to reduce the deficit. The combined effects of slower growth and higher taxes have been dramatic. Disposable family incomes after inflation grew 34 percent in the 1960s, 22 percent in the 1970s and only 0.5 percent in the 1980s. And this squeeze will continue because growth will be slow and taxes will have to go up more. Little wonder citizens are irritable and insecure.

While our slower growth had a profound effect on all aspects of Canadian life, we did not adjust to it. It was less painful to ignore it. The expectations formed in the 1970s, during high real growth rates, were not sustainable in the 1980s with lower growth rates. Our failure to adjust expectations in part explains the fiscal crisis. We kept demanding improved and expanded public services as in the 1970s, yet would not pay the sharp tax increases necessary in a time of slower growth. The accumulated debt ballooned. The future adjustment will be doubly wrenching.

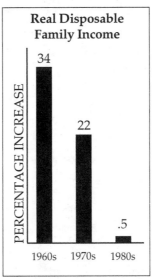

Source: Income After Tax (Statistics Canada 13-210)

In the past, Canada's abundant raw materials have given it an advantage in world markets. But world prices for primary products have been in long-term decline and just as our new sources of supply are becoming more costly to develop, other countries around the world are bringing lower-cost sources into production. Our traditional ace in the hole — the value of our resource base — is diminishing and Canada's trade must increasingly be in manufacturing and services. This is already happening. During the 1980s non-resource–based exports rose from 38 to 49 percent of total trade.

Our prosperity is closely linked to the rate of increase in productivity. In our local economy we prosper if productivity, or output per hour of work, increases. Productivity growth is somewhat affected by government policies but is largely determined at the level of the individual enterprise and depends on the skill of management, the level of invest-

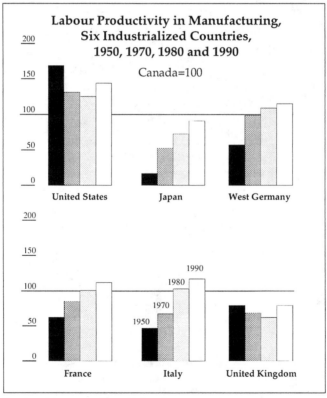

Based on data measured in output per hour
Source: A Joint Venture, 1991 ECC Annual Review

ment in productive capital, the technology used and the quality of the labour force. Productivity growth means prosperity not just from production at home but also from international trade. More competitors are entering international markets, and our success will increasingly depend on productivity growth and innovation.

At the moment, this is hardly our strong suit. Canada has been in a productivity slowdown, indeed our productivity growth has been declining over the last three decades and remains below both the OECD and G-7 average. The problems are most acute in manufacturing, the sector that accounts for the bulk of world trade. During the 1980s our manufacturing productivity declined relative to that of the U.S. while France, West Germany and Italy all moved ahead of us.

The globalization of the world economy is transforming both national economies and national politics. Consumers in Canada and around the world are aware of product standards in the global marketplace and demand the same for themselves — whether these products are Italian fashion, Japanese cars or American computer software. Their demands are pressing down trade barriers and even overthrowing political regimes. This openness is a two-way street, as we get access to foreign products, foreign producers get access to our markets. An immediate result of globalization is concern about the competitiveness of our manufacturing industries.

One important aspect of competitiveness is labour costs. During the 1980s our labour costs rose an alarming 39 percent compared to the U.S. Since the Canada-U.S. exchange rate was roughly unchanged over the decade, this deterioration was because our productivity grew more slowly and wages grew faster.

It is not as if we have not long recognized the structural and productivity problems of the Canadian economy: too much export of natural resources without further processing; research and development spending far below most advanced countries; technology-based industries underrepresented in our industrial structure; skills education in the school and in the workplace that is below our competitors'; public policies that impede rather than encourage adjustment; and labour market policies that give little incentive for retraining or mobility. Recognize it we can; respond to it we cannot.

Our response to the emerging global challenge has been tentative and indecisive. Some people are arguing that the existing constitutional structure has impeded our response. Whatever one believes, it is clear neither level of government has primary responsibility or mandate to develop a response. Many Québécois believe they could prosper more as a sovereign country than within Canada.

Another aspect of economic performance is macroeconomic — how closely the economy operates to full employment and to the capacity of its physical capital without triggering an acceleration of inflation. This macroeconomic performance can also influence productivity growth. If unemployment is high, people have less incentive to retrain. They adopt an attitude of defeat: Why bother? There are no jobs anyway. High inflation distorts investment decision making. It is costly and difficult to adjust to high and uncertain rates of inflation because market signals are hard to read and greater returns are made in financial investments that are redistributions, rather than real investments that increase national output.

Canada had a poorer macroeconomic record than most industrialized countries during the 1980s. We have had both higher unemployment *and* higher inflation.

Transitions for the 90s, the 1990 Annual Review of the Economic Council of Canada, was a pointed analysis of these problems. It identified two major transitions that will be crucial to the performance of the Canadian economy over the longer term. The first has already been discussed: productivity improvement and adjustment as our economy becomes more integrated into the global economy. The second is to find better ways to reduce unemployment while controlling inflation. "To reduce unemployment, we must find ways to improve the capacity of Canadians to adapt to the dramatic changes in the world economy. We must also find ways to control inflation that do not involve periodic bouts of policy restraint that cause setbacks on employment, investment and sales."

Our mix of economic growth, fiscal and monetary policies has created a growing reliance on foreign borrowing. Our current account deficit relative to GDP is now the largest among the G-7 countries and balance-of-payments problems are looming.

Many of our labour market and business assistance programs actually discourage adjustment and make macroeconomic policy more difficult. Take for example the unemployment insurance program. While receiving payments an individual must look for a job in his or her own field and area, but is not offered training or relocation services. Too often our business assistance programs preserve a way of a life rather than encourage efficiency. Both business and labour are too dependent on government transfers and too accepting of existing arrangements. More self-reliance, more innovation, more use of new technologies, management practices and compensation systems are necessary. Our wages must be more responsive to economic conditions. We need more coordinated fiscal policies among levels of government and better coordination of monetary and fiscal policy.

Historically, fiscal and monetary policy have been the responsibility of the federal government, but because provincial-local expenditure areas have grown more rapidly over the last few decades, the aggregate of provincial fiscal policies is greater than federal fiscal policy. And regions are now demanding a voice in setting monetary policy. Improved macroeconomic performance will require that we address this new situation, perhaps through constitutional changes.

The Future of Social Programs

We want a higher national income not for its own sake but for what it can provide us. We want higher incomes not only to house, clothe, feed and entertain ourselves but also for better education, health care and social services. Our third economic challenge is to secure the future of our social programs.

The fiscal crisis, our threatened future prosperity and our future social programs are all intertwined. Without future prosperity, we will have lower private consumption and fewer public services. Meeting the fiscal crisis will require expenditure restraint. This awareness is more and more widely shared. Yet many Canadians fear that in our attempts to deal with deficits and competitiveness, we are abandoning our most prized accomplishments of the last thirty years and transforming what it means to be a Canadian. Their vision of Canada is being stolen from them.

From the postwar period into the early 1970s, Canadians put in place an array of social programs that were the envy of much of the world. The heart of the Canadian welfare state is in education, health and social services including unemployment insurance, pensions and income security. Primary and secondary education is universal and free, and there is an extensive system of colleges and universities receiving over 80 percent of their funds from the public sector. Health care is universal and free. The Unemployment Insurance Program and the Canada Pension Plan are comprehensive. Income security is provided through the old age pension, the guaranteed income supplement, spouses allowances, family allowances, child tax credits and welfare. Together, education, health and social services represent about one half of all government spending, and about 60 percent of expenditure excluding payments on the debt.

Each country has chosen its own mix of public and private activity in their economy. Canada is slightly below the G-7 and OECD averages of social spending as a percentage of GDP. But our spending on education and health is above average for industrialized countries.

During most of the postwar period there was a broad consensus supporting the developing welfare state. It seemed consistent with a Keynesian approach to macroeconomic policy in which governments pursued full employment and stable prices using fiscal and monetary policy; social insurance was regarded as a right of citizenship. Social science held the promise that government programs could solve or at least alleviate problems of delinquency, family violence, poverty and discrimination. Social policy and economic policy went hand in hand into a better future. High-quality public services and social justice were not only a dividend from a prosperous economy, they were a necessary complement to the smooth operation of a market economy.

Things changed during the 1980s. The fiscal crisis emerged and became worse despite our attempts to control it. Finally the government acted: the federal budget of February 1990 introduced an explicit expenditure control plan. A number of programs were frozen for two years, including the transfers to the provinces used to pay for health and post-secondary education. Other programs were limited to a 5

percent annual growth for two years including federal transfers that share the cost of social welfare assistance to Ontario,
Alberta and British Columbia. (Major federal transfers to
people, such as old age pensions, unemployment insurance
and Indian and Inuit programs, were exempted from the control plan.) The budget of February 1991 extended these
expenditure controls for a further two years.

The federal government strategy, to pass some of the fiscal
crisis on to the provincial level, is obvious. Less obvious is
how much it will weaken the national commitment to health
care, post-secondary education and social welfare. Of course,
provinces could raise taxes to make up the difference and
maintain services, but the basic components of the welfare
state are no longer being fully supported at the federal level.
This in itself was a radical change in direction for Canada.

Strategies to increase competitiveness and future prosperity have charted a new course, which is alarming to many.
Deregulation seemed to mean a reduced commitment to social concerns, freer trade brought the cold shower of
competition but no adjustment assistance, and reduced inflation was purchased with a severe and prolonged recession.

The postwar consensus about the welfare state has fragmented. Several macroeconomic schools vie to replace
Keynesianism. Vocal opponents of increasing the level of social protection grow more powerful and social scientists are
less sanguine about their abilities to diagnose and treat social
ills. Some even assert that our previous attempts to cure
society's ills have actually made things worse. Perhaps the
most fundamental change in attitude is the increasingly popu-
lar notion that social policy and economic policy are no longer
complementary. Social services have become an expensive,
bureaucratic drag on economic activity.

Despite this fragmented consensus and our economic
problems, the Canadian welfare state has *not* been rolled back.
In contrast to the United States and the United Kingdom, our
income distribution has not become more unequal over the
1980s. It is clear that Canadians still place a high value on
social programs. The Citizens' Forum on Canada's Future
reported "participants deeply value Canada's compassionate
and generous character, as exemplified by our universal and
extensive social services, our health care system, our pen-

sions, our willingness to welcome refugees and our commitment to regional equalization. These attributes are most
definitely seen as part of Canada's distinct character."

What Should Be in a Constitution?

Our constitutional dilemma has dragged on for twenty years.
Maybe our constitutional wrangling has stopped us from
dealing with our economic problems. Maybe the economic
issues are so threatening that constitution making should be
set aside until economic security is restored.

Appealing as that argument may be, it has no practical
relevance. Constitutional reform cannot be put aside. Neither
Quebec nor the West nor aboriginal peoples would accept it.

Indeed, there are more compelling arguments that constitutional change must be part of a solution to our economic
problems. Without a constitution — without stable rules of
the game — neither the public sector nor the private sector can
confront economic issues properly.

Another argument is that Canada is too regionalized for a
national strategy and that federal power has hampered local
initiatives. It is alleged that increased provincial power
would permit more creative responses to our productivity
problems and allow redesign of our social programs. Provincial control would remove the wasteful duplication and turf
wars in our existing federal-provincial arrangements. This
argument was central to the call for radical devolution of
power to Quebec by the Quebec Liberal Party in the Allaire
Report.

The opposing approach focuses on a constitutional
strengthening of the economic union as a means to secure our
economic prosperity. An economic union implies the free
flow of people, goods, services, and capital — the so-called
four freedoms. It also means uniform business framework
laws and coordinated economic and tax policies among the
provinces. The 1991 federal document — *Shaping Canada's
Future Together: Proposals* — focuses on enhancing the economic union to secure future prosperity.

Yet another approach emphasizes that a constitution is not
just the division of power and the rules of the economic game,
but a statement of shared values. A recommitment to shared
values is a necessary basis for confronting economic adjust-

ment. A social charter in the constitution would, it is argued, protect and guarantee social programs such as universal education and medicare. Because economic change might alter our social programs, this approach would entrench commitments to them in our constitution.

Indeed, Canadians do not seem to be saying the constitution is irrelevant to our economic problems. It is quite the reverse. We are trying to solve all our problems through constitutional reform — and all at once. We are confusing the rules of the game with the play of the game. Everyday decisions that should be made by citizens and politicians in the political process are being debated in the constitutional arena.

Constitutions should be flexible enough to allow for the fact that what governments do changes over time, in ways which are quite unforeseen. For example, most of what governments now do was not anticipated when our constitution was written in 1867. The need for flexibility is especially important as Canadians have such complex and conflicting national and regional aspirations. It is foolhardy to entrench ideas that do not command consensus. Our diversity must be accommodated.

The constitutional treatment of economic ideas should recognize what governments actually do and are expected to do. The Canadian economy is a mixed economy with substantial roles for the public, private and third sectors. Each is legitimate, but we will always be shifting the desired balance among them. The objectives of government are multi-dimensional and there will always be overlaps between the jurisdictions of the federal and provincial levels, just as there are overlaps in the jurisdictions of different government departments. Constitutions cannot divide powers into watertight compartments.

A new constitution is not magic. It will not solve all our economic problems or resolve all our alternative visions. But if we craft a reform that achieves legitimacy and acceptability in all parts of the country, we might just get better government. This is not to say all tensions will disappear. Such is not the nature of modern societies. We cannot create one vision from many; we can only learn to live with them.

2

Our Existing Federal System

How many of us understand the existing constitution? What are our national institutions? What is the division of powers between federal and provincial governments? What is the role of equalization? How are social programs paid for, and how are economic affairs managed? We must understand our existing federal system before we discuss changes.

Our federal system of government was first set out in the *British North America Act, 1867* and has been amended many times since. The most recent amendment was the *Constitution Act, 1982*, which contains the *Canadian Charter of Rights and Freedoms*; at the same time the entire constitution was patriated. Collectively, these acts are consolidated as the *Constitution Acts, 1867 to 1982*. This is the constitution we want to change.

The constitution creates legislative, executive and judicial branches for the nation and for each province. Both the national government, which we now call the federal government, and the provincial governments have independent sovereignty. National issues are to be handled by the sovereign national institutions, not through coordination among the provinces.

The national legislative institution is the Parliament of Canada made up of the House of Commons and the Senate. The Commons has 295 members elected from across Canada, with the numbers from each province roughly proportional to the population. The Commons is the supreme legislative body and must originate all money bills. The Senate usually has 104 members, appointed nominally by the governor general although actually by the prime minister. The Senate was designed to be regionally representative and is made up of four equal-sized divisions plus six senators from Newfoundland and one each from the Yukon Territory and the Northwest Territories. The four divisions, each with twenty-four senators, are Ontario, Quebec, the Maritime provinces (Nova Scotia, New Brunswick and Prince Edward Island) and the western provinces (Manitoba, Saskatchewan, Alberta and British Columbia). The Senate has obviously failed to represent regional concerns in national institutions, partly because it is unelected and therefore without effective voice in legislative matters and partly because the number of senators from each province does not properly counteract a representation based on population. As would be appropriate, Ontario has a smaller proportion of senators than its proportion of population, but Alberta also has a proportion of senators less than its population share. Small wonder the loudest calls for Senate reform come from that province.

Representation in the
Parliament of Canada by Province

	Share of Population	Share of House of Commons Members	Share of Senators
Newfoundland	2.2	2.4	5.8
Prince Edward Island	0.5	1.4	3.8
Nova Scotia	3.4	3.7	9.6
New Brunswick	2.7	3.4	9.6
Quebec	25.4	25.4	23.1
Ontario	36.6	32.2	23.1
Manitoba	4.1	6.4	5.8
Saskatchewan	3.8	4.7	5.8
Alberta	9.3	8.8	5.8
British Columbia	11.8	10.8	5.8
Yukon	0.1	0.3	1.0
Northwest Territories	0.2	0.7	1.0
	100.0	100.0	100.0

Division of Powers

The division of powers in the constitution is specified in Sections 91, 92 and 93 of the *British North America Act*. This was a mid-nineteenth century document and of course reflects a mid-nineteenth century view of the appropriate activities of government. Much of what government does today is not explicitly mentioned in the division of powers, but the constitution has proven quite flexible and our domain of government differs little from other countries with different constitutions.

Section 91 establishes the legislative authority of the Parliament of Canada. It can make laws for the "peace, order and good government of Canada" and in all matters not assigned exclusively to the provinces. Thus the federal government has what is termed "the residual power" — an important sphere of sovereignty as the role of government evolves. For greater certainty, the section also sets out matters that are the exclusive authority of the federal government including public debt and property, regulation of trade and commerce, currency and coinage, the issuance of paper money and savings banks. The Parliament of Canada is also responsible for the postal service, the census, defence and foreign affairs, navigation shipping and transportation systems that link provinces, the sea coast and inland fisheries, criminal law and penitentiaries. In 1940 the constitution was amended making unemployment insurance a federal responsibility and in 1951 an amendment allowed federal laws for old age pensions (continuing to allow present or future provincial old age pension laws). The federal Parliament can raise money by any mode or system of taxation.

Section 92 establishes the exclusive sovereignty of the provinces; in general they are to deal with "all matters of a merely local or private nature in the province." The listed areas of exclusive provincial sovereignty include public lands, timber, hospitals and asylums, municipal institutions, local public works, property and civil rights, and the administration of both civil and criminal law in the province. An amendment was added in 1982, giving provinces exclusive responsibility for non-renewable natural resources (oil, gas and minerals), forestry resources and electrical energy. Provinces can only raise money through direct taxation.

Section 93 gives provinces exclusive responsibility for education, subject to the rights Protestant, Catholic and other denominational schools had at the time of Confederation.

The provinces and the federal government have concurrent powers in agriculture and immigration, but in cases of dispute federal law is supreme.

The creation of Canada in 1867 brought together three colonial provinces: Canada (which included Upper and Lower Canada), Nova Scotia and New Brunswick. The constitutional preamble says "such a Union would conduce to the welfare of the provinces and promote the interests of the British Empire" — but it is clear the French should have a special place. To accommodate and protect the French fact, Quebec was created. Consequently, the new nation had a national government and four provincial governments — Ontario, Quebec, Nova Scotia and New Brunswick.

The role for government envisioned at the time was rather limited. Most of the population was rural, engaged in self-sufficient agriculture. Even in the 1880s, over 60 percent of the population lived on farms. Travel between provinces was difficult. Trade was conducted by water. Local trade was quite limited while international trade sent furs, fish and lumber to Europe in exchange for manufactured goods. The main source of government revenue was customs and excise duties. In this world the federal government was responsible for national institutions, defence and international trade and for developing a national economy. Of course, the provincial economies were quite independent then, but the vision was to integrate them, especially by federally provided infrastructure. The original constitution even had a "common market" clause; Section 121 reads "All articles of the growth, produce or manufacture of any one of the provinces shall, from and after the union, be admitted free into each of the other provinces." The provinces would provide the municipal institutions, local courts, local public works and limited hospitals, asylums and education that were envisaged for a rural nineteenth-century society.

This constitutional division of powers set out in 1867 has remained, with modest amendment, despite enormous changes in Canadian society. The nation expanded to the Pacific Ocean and the West was settled, swelling the total population from 3.2 million in 1861 to 7.2 million in 1911. Then Canada urbanized and industrialized. In the postwar period, urbanization continued and our economy shifted into services. Today about 65 percent of our 26.6 million people live in our 27 census metropolitan areas. Only 3 percent of employment is in agriculture while 16 percent is in manufacturing and 71 percent is in services. Probably the most dramatic change of all is the steady rise in income: since 1951, real per capita income has almost tripled.

Throughout this period and especially since the 1940s, the role of government was transformed in two separate but interrelated ways. First, the government assumed responsibility for the management of the economy. The ideas of Keynes held sway. Voters increasingly used the level of unemployment, the rate of inflation and the rate of economic growth to judge the performance of government. Primary responsibility fell to the federal government, although macroeconomic policy was certainly not mentioned in the constitution. Second, the government began to provide more social services. Education and health care expanded; an income security system based on family allowances, old age pensions, unemployment insurance and welfare was put in place; and governments strove to reduce inequalities in income between people, regions and provinces. Most of these activities fell in provincial jurisdiction. Total government spending (including debt charges) was 20 percent of the economy in 1950 and now stands at 44 percent. It casts no aspersions on the wisdom of the Fathers of Confederation to say they did not anticipate these transformations.

Federal–Provincial Fiscal Relations

These two transformations put pressure on the Canadian federal system defined by the constitution. In the 1950s, following its enlarged role in the Depression and the war, the federal government was fiscally dominant. The dominance increased because of the government's responsibility to manage the economy through fiscal and monetary policy. Yet the growing expenditure areas were provincial. What emerged was a complex system of federal–provincial fiscal relations, characterized by three major components: tax collection agreements, the federal spending power and transfers from the federal to provincial governments. Today, federal spending excluding transfers to the provinces (but including debt charges) is only 40 percent of total government spending. Ottawa is not the dominant level, at least in expenditure terms.

Although the constitution appears to restrict the taxing powers of the provinces, limiting them to direct taxes, the restrictions are more apparent than real. Sales and excise taxes are regarded as indirect taxes and constitutionally outside provincial jurisdiction. But the provinces have successfully argued that their sales and excise taxes are not levied on the retailer (to be passed indirectly to the purchaser), rather sales taxes are levied on the purchaser and are collected by the retailer on behalf of the province. Both federal and provincial governments occupy the personal and corporate income tax fields as well as the sales and excise fields. During World War II, the federal government took over the personal and corporate income tax bases under wartime tax rental agreements.

A series of tax collection agreements for both personal and corporate income taxes evolved out of the wartime experience. Under the personal income tax agreements, provinces accept the federal base and rate structure, but choose their

Federal Payments to Provinces 1989-90 ($ millions)

	EPF Cash Transfers	EPF Tax Transfers	CAP Cash Transfers	Equalization Cash Transfers	Share of Provincial Revenues from Federal Transfers
Newfoundland	214	107	103	941	47
Prince Edward Island	49	28	24	203	45
Nova Scotia	334	233	173	918	40
New Brunswick	271	165	170	903	40
Quebec	1,461	3,047	1,134	3,866	20
Ontario	2,931	4,235	1,946	--	13
Manitoba	409	287	210	884	29
Saskatchewan	381	242	172	494	23
Alberta	929	884	534	--	15
British Columbia	1,212	1,073	737	--	17
Yukon	18	21	15	--	71
Northwest Territories	9	9	5	--	84
Total	8,217	10,330	5,223	8,209	

Sources: The National Finances 1990, Table 16.2 and Provincial Economic Accounts (Statistics Canada 13-213)

own rates as a percentage of federal taxes payable. The federal government administers the tax collection and auditing, and turns the money over to the provinces. It will also administer limited special provincial provisions. All provinces, except Quebec, have signed personal income tax agreements with Ottawa. The corporate tax agreements also accept the federal base, but each province applies its own rate to the common base. Alberta, Quebec and Ontario have not signed corporate tax collection agreements, but their tax bases do not differ significantly from the federal base.

Sharing tax fields and a high degree of harmonization has meant that funds could be transferred up to the federal level, as in wartime, and back down to the provincial level by a re-arrangement of tax rates. For example the federal government can transfer funds to the province by reducing its tax rate, giving the province tax room. The province can then raise its rates and acquire money to finance expenditure.

The federal spending power is the second component of federal–provincial fiscal relations. The constitution sets out clear areas of provincial responsibility including health, education and welfare. But the federal government has always held that other constitutional clauses allow it to make direct cash payments to provinces, institutions or individuals in areas of *exclusive provincial jurisdiction*. This is the so-called federal spending power. Use of the power allowed the country to escape the conundrum of a fiscally dominant central government juxtaposed against growing provincial expenditure responsibilities. The federal government initiated shared-cost programs in many areas including health, post-secondary education and welfare, often placing conditions on the funds in order to shape provincial expenditure patterns.

The federal spending power has created a complicated system of transfers from the federal to provincial governments. The terms of transfer have been constantly evolving, especially since the mid 1960s when provinces, led by Quebec, demanded more control of these expenditure fields. In 1964, the federal government allowed provinces to opt out of these shared-cost programs, granting financial compensation to the province if the province provided a roughly similar program with the money. The Quebec government immediately opted out of twenty-eight federal programs. The largest current federal-provincial transfers are the Established Programs Financing system and the Canada Assistance Plan, although there are dozens of other programs.

The Established Programs Financing (EPF) system was developed in 1977 to replace a shared-cost program for health and post-secondary education. Under the old shared-cost system, the federal government would split each dollar of spending with the provinces according to a pre-arranged ratio. In contrast, the new EPF was a block grant system. The change was designed to reduce some of the constraints on provincial spending under the shared-cost system and to stop the open-ended financial commitment of the federal government. The EPF transfer consists of a cash grant and a transfer of tax room under the income tax agreements. The federal government retained the cash component to allow it some leverage in how the money is spent. It is thus able to assert national standards and make benefits under these programs a part of national citizenship. However these national standards are always staunchly resisted by Quebec.

Section 36

(1)Without altering the legislative authority of Parliament or of the provincial legislatures, or the rights of any of them with respect to the exercise of their legislative authority, Parliament and the legislatures, together with the government of Canada and the provincial governments, are committed to

    (a)promoting equal opportunities for the well-being of Canadians

    (b)furthering economic development to reduce disparities in opportunities; and

    (c)providing essential public services of reasonable quality to all Canadians.

(2)Parliament and the government of Canada are committed to the principle of making equalization payments to ensure that provincial governments have sufficient revenues to provide reasonably comparable levels of public services at reasonably comparable levels of taxation.

Source: The Constitution Act, 1982

The Canada Assistance Plan (CAP), which finances provincial welfare programs and the operating costs of some provincial social services, remains a shared-cost program. The federal government pays 50 percent of the cost. Provincial programs must meet federal conditions, most importantly that residency requirements are not too strict. Again, federal leverage is used to pursue a national objective: facilitating mobility across the country.

Equalization Payments are another major federal transfer program. The government transfers federally raised funds to have-not provinces. The transfers flow to provinces whose tax capacities fall short of the average tax capacities of British Columbia, Saskatchewan, Manitoba, Ontario and Quebec. Usually all but three provinces — British Columbia, Alberta and Ontario — receive equalization grants.

These federal contributions to equalization and social programs, after operating for years under vague constitutional justification, were entrenched in Section 36 of the *Constitution Act, 1982*. Although few people recognize it, the section can be considered a social charter, or at least the strong beginnings of one.

The constitutional division of powers is always a constraint on government policy in Canada, but compartments are never watertight. We have always managed to accommodate new government responsibilities and to balance national citizenship against local autonomy through judicious use of the federal spending power, intergovernmental grants and administrative arrangements. The results are never without controversy and the balance is always shifting, but this is inherent in the citizen's dual loyalties under a federal system.

Economic Union

Canada's strong commitments to equalization and comparable service levels across the country were formalized in the 1982 constitutional amendment. They are in part an implementation of our national vision and also in part a recognition that the benefits from our integrated economy should be shared across the nation. We are wealthier together than separate, and this extra wealth should be shared.

Today, driven by the social, political and economic forces of globalization, nations around the world are integrating their economies with other nations', sometimes slowly, sometimes rapidly, but always inexorably. Among nations there are various levels of integration. Under a free-trade zone, all tariffs on the movement of goods and services between nations are removed. Canada is entering this level of integration with the United States. The next level of integration is a customs union. Within the union is a free-trade zone. The participating nations agree to impose common tariffs on goods entering from outside the zone. A common market extends the integration to include the free mobility of labour and capital. An economic union is a common market with harmonization of economic and even social policy. It is sometimes said that creation of a common market is negative integration — the removal of barriers — whereas the creation of an economic union is positive integration — the harmonization of policies. A monetary union adds the element of a common currency among nations.

Most of Europe is, today, a common market moving toward an economic and monetary union. Such close economic integration inevitably brings political integration, and a European political union is being explored. However they have not yet addressed how to redistribute the gains from integration.

Within a single nation, these levels of integration have less meaning. Nations are economic unions, monetary unions and of course political unions. Canada is no exception. However, in federal states powers are divided among several governments, and there is always a concern that the economic union will be fragmented. Almost everyone believes the Canadian economic union should be preserved and enhanced. The many benefits of economic integration are well recognized. Companies and people become more efficient; resources can move to their most productive location; the risks and volatility of a small specialized economy are spread over a larger more diversified one; large fixed costs for such things as defence, external affairs and research can be borne across a larger number of people; and larger nations have more clout and are better able to defend their interests in international affairs.

If we look at the Canadian economy and consider the mobility of labour, of goods and services, and of capital and consider the harmonization of economic and social policies, we find our economic union quite complete. However there remain barriers, caused by both provincial and federal governments.

Canada has relatively free mobility of labour within its boundaries, and what a benefit this is. How many of us are now living and working in the province where we were born? Our children's horizons would be very confined if they had to go to school and find work only in the province of their birth. During the 1980s, an average of 320,000 people changed provinces each year. As people move to where they can be more productive, both personal and national income rises. This labour mobility helps Canada adjust to the economic shocks that strike different regions of the country.

Some labour barriers remain, erected by both the federal and provincial governments. Provinces have different occupational licensing and on occasion have hiring preferences for their own people. The federal unemployment insurance system has regionally differentiated benefits that reduce labour mobility.

Goods and services also move easily across the country. Since Confederation, the common market clause has forbidden interprovincial tariffs. About two-thirds of provincial gross output is sold in the province while 20 percent is sold in other provinces and 18 percent outside the country. (Gross output is a measure of all output, including intermediate and final goods and therefore is greater than GDP. Exports are 25 percent of Canadian GDP.) Thus interprovincial trade is more important than international trade in Canada. To put it in perspective, Canadian interprovincial trade is a greater share of total output than trade among nations in the European Community. The degree of interconnection between provinces depends on their resource base, economic structure, history and geography. Ontario and Quebec for instance, have strong ties with each other and although all of the other provinces have strong trade ties with Ontario and Quebec, trade links within and between other regions are weak.

The redirected trade flows following the Canada-U.S. Free Trade Agreement and globalization are felt by some analysts to be eroding the linkages across Canada. However, recent research by the Economic Council of Canada suggests this is not the case. International ties are growing and so the importance of the local provincial market is diminishing, but cross-country ties have not been weakened.

Barriers to the free movement of goods and services remain. Provincial government procurement policies and provincial policies on beer and wine are examples. But federal policies that prevent goods from being produced at their most efficient location or that favour one sort of production (e.g., atomic energy) over another (e.g., hydroelectricity) also prevent the free and efficient allocation of resources. The CF-18 maintenance contract and the Crow's Nest Pass freight rates are notorious examples.

Capital is extraordinarily mobile across the country, greatly assisted by our national banking system, although there remain tax preferences for in-province investments and financial regulations that differ across the country.

Our economic union is also tremendously enhanced by the harmonization of our federal, provincial and local tax systems. Our tax systems have been organized, specifically through the tax collection agreements, to reduce the costs of collection and compliance and to ensure that people and firms are subject to roughly the same rules wherever they live. This ensures mobility, fairness, and administrative efficiency, as well as ensuring that people and firms work where they are most productive. But this harmonization is in danger of breaking down. More and more special provisions are being introduced into provincial tax systems. Many provinces are considering opting out of the tax collection agreements and, most worryingly, the federal government introduced the Goods and Services Tax (GST) without securing harmonization with provincial sales taxes. When the federal government was dominant financially, its fiscal policy was national fiscal policy. But as the provincial sector grew, so did the importance of provincial fiscal policies. In recent years, federal and provincial budgets have sometimes worked at cross purposes.

Certainly at the level of negative integration, the Canadian economic union is quite complete. It is less complete in the harmonization of policies that constitute positive integration. Many of the gains from Canadian integration have been realized already. Only modest further benefits are likely. In spite

of wide recognition of our gains from integration, recent political trends and now our constitutional proposals threaten
the existing union. The losses from a fragmented union could
be enormous.

Internal Barriers to Trade

Barriers to the Free Flow of Goods and Services
Government procurement policies
Agricultural marketing boards and support programs
Provincial policies on beer and wine
Technical norms and product standards
Transportation regulations and subsidies
   (e.g., Western Grain Transportation Act)
Resource policies (e.g., processing and exploration policies)
Government subsidies (e.g., export subsidies and tax
concessions)

Barriers to the Free Flow of Labour
Occupational licensing and certification
Preferential hiring practices
Non-portability of private pension plans
Regionally differentiated unemployment insurance benefits

Barriers to the Free Flow of Capital
Tax preferences for in-province investments
Controls on land purchases
Restrictions on the portfolios of investment funds
   and financial institutions
Enterprise zones
Industrial incentives and subsidies

Source: A Joint Venture, 1991 ECC Annual Review

3

One Country:
Alternative Federal Structures

The late 1970s were a period of intense constitutional discussion in Canada. The Parti Québécois was elected in 1976. The West grew more assertive during that period, demanding greater control over its resources and economic development. Overall, Canadians sensed minor changes here and there would not be enough to ensure the country's survival. The government of René Lévesque pressed ahead with a referendum asking for a mandate to negotiate sovereignty-association for Quebec. The Quebec premier, in the bitterest defeat of his political career, lost the referendum and had to acknowledge the people of Quebec had given federalism another chance. Now it was up to the federalists "to put content to the promises they rained upon us. They all said that if the NO won, the status quo was dead and buried."

Unfinished Business
In the wake of the referendum, Prime Minister Trudeau and the ten premiers met and drew up a list of twelve issues for discussion over the summer. A monograph entitled *A Citizen's Guide to the Constitutional Question* was published in1980. It discussed the twelve issues and still makes interesting reading. Canada has much unfinished business.

The *Constitution Act, 1982* was the result of meetings of the eleven governments. The constitution was finally patriated after 115 years and an amending formula was adopted. The

Act included the *Canadian Charter of Rights and Freedoms,* a section on aboriginal rights and Section 36, which deals with equalization and regional disparities. The provinces won unambiguous jurisdiction over non-renewable natural resources, forestry resources and electric energy. But the new constitution did not have the agreement of the Parti Québécois government in Quebec City.

The Charter has forever altered the relationship between citizen and government in Canada. We have shifted away from the British tradition where the rule of law under a sovereign Parliament protects the civil liberties of Canadians, toward a U.S. tradition where citizens' rights are prior to and above the will of government. The Charter protects against encroachments by government and is enforceable through the courts.

Although many of these changes were momentous, a re-reading of the twelve discussion items shows what was left out. Almost no changes were made to the division of powers although it was discussed. Those who sought more powers for province building, especially in Quebec, were disappointed. The federal spending power, so long contentious between Ottawa and the provinces, was not clarified. Since 1982, the pressures to grant the provinces more powers have increased manyfold.

In 1982, the means to secure the economic union was a major agenda item, but all that emerged was a section on mobility rights in the Charter. For some time, it had been recognized that as the provincial share of government spending had grown, Ottawa's ability to conduct fiscal policy had diminished. Only with coordinated federal and provincial budgets could the national economy be managed. Also the need for greater harmonization of labour and business framework laws was acknowledged. But no mechanism to deal with it was put in place.

Most critically, however, the 1982 constitution reenforced one vision of Canada. It was the Pan-Canadian vision. It begins from the proposition that the nation as a whole is most important. Canada is a union of its people, not a pact among ten sovereign provinces. The central tasks of the national government are international affairs, managing the national economy, redistributing the income and wealth of the country, and forging and sustaining the common identity and common values of all Canadians. All citizens are equal under the Charter. All provinces are equal in their powers.

But there are other visions as well. And the vision expressed in 1982 has not solidified into a national consensus. During the mid 1980s, our constitutional evolution continued with an attempt to secure the government of Quebec's "inclusion into the constitutional family" that culminated in the Meech Lake Accord. The Accord embodied the five conditions necessary for Quebec's acceptance: recognition of Quebec as a distinct society, a Quebec veto on changes to national institutions, restrictions on the federal spending power, increased Quebec power over immigration and three Quebec judges on the Supreme Court. It was clear that Quebec planned to use the distinct society clause to obtain greater powers, but the Accord made no explicit change to the division of powers. The Accord also committed the federal government to holding annual first ministers' conferences on the economy. Despite the agreement of the prime minister and ten premiers in 1987, the Accord could not pass all ten provincial legislatures by the three-year deadline.

Quebec's vision continued to evolve after the collapse of Meech and is now articulated in the Allaire Report, *A Québec Free to Choose*, adopted by the Quebec Liberal Party. "In Quebec, confederation has always been perceived as a solemn pact between two nations." Quebec is the national state of French-Canadians and English Canada is the other nation state. The Allaire Report implies Québécois have almost exclusive loyalty to Quebec. The Quebec Liberal Party proposes a new Quebec-Canada structure with complete political autonomy for Quebec. Our current national institutions would be largely abolished. "A common political structure will be created, with responsibilities for consultation, coordination and execution in the areas of authority to be delegated to it where an association between Quebec and Canada proves to be mutually beneficial." This common political structure would scarcely be a national government; its delegated responsibilities would be limited.

A second vision stresses the equality of the provinces and considers Canada to be a union of the provinces. This idea of a community of communities and of province building has been most strongly expressed by the western provinces, especially Alberta, but is also heard in the Maritimes. Province builders want greater decentralization in both economic and social policy as well as greater provincial voice in federal decisions that affect them. Canada would be strong because each province was strong.

Each of these visions of Canada recognizes dual loyalties — to the part and the whole. The balance of the loyalties implies a different constitutional structure in each. Each carries implications for the division of powers, equalization payments and social programs, management of the economic union, and design of national institutions. The vision of native Canadians implies a third federal model, but we do not yet know enough about the meaning of "aboriginal self-government" to set out the constitutional and economic implications.

The 1991 Federal Proposals

The Pan-Canadian vision dominated during the postwar period. Our existing federalism reflects this, although it has made concessions to Quebec and to province-building pressures. Now, there seems consensus that some sort of further decentralization is necessary and the federal government itself no longer champions the Canada-centred vision.

However, there are important, though disparate, groups in sympathy with a Pan-Canadian vision. There are nationalists who view Canadian history as a long struggle to create a nation, at first different from Britain and now different from the United States. They want a strong central government to protect and develop our distinctiveness. Those focusing on the economic union and the importance of international trading negotiations often recommend a strong central government. Similar recommendations often come from those emphasizing the need to entrench Canadian values in a social charter. The vision of a bilingual Canada usually implies a strong national role. Smaller provinces fear a weakened central government would be less committed to equalization. But these groups have not succeeded in allying to offer a specific constitutional proposal to Canadians.

The federal position released in the fall of 1991 — *Shaping Canada's Future Together: Proposals* — attempts to accommodate several visions. The proposals would recognize Quebec as a distinct society; create an elected and effective Senate with more equitable provincial and territorial representation; create a Council of the Federation made up of federal, provincial and territorial governments; and recognize the right to aboriginal self-government. As under the Meech Lake Accord, the unanimous consent of Parliament and the provinces would be required for amendments affecting federal institutions. It does not, however, propose a specific reconciliation of the visions. Instead it sets out a framework for continuing dialogue between Ottawa and the provinces. This explains why some people regard the proposals as a massive federal power grab while others see catastrophic decentralization. Both are predicting what will evolve under the framework. But perhaps this is the best we can hope for in a constitution for our diverse nation: a framework for political forces to shape our country.

The federal proposals contain modest specific suggestions for decentralization. Labour market training, tourism, forestry, mining, recreation, housing and municipal-urban affairs are recommended as areas of exclusive provincial jurisdiction. The document suggests shared jurisdiction over immigration and culture and there would be studies of how to streamline federal and provincial programs in a number of areas, to provide the best service at the lowest possible cost.

The proposals provide the opportunity for far more decentralization. A constitutional amendment is proposed to allow legislative delegation of powers between Parliament and the legislatures with their mutual consent. A national government could arrange to devolve substantial powers to Quebec without involving the other provinces. But by the same token a group of provinces could agree to pass power up to Ottawa, and not all provinces would have to participate.

The federal spending power would be formalized in the constitution. It could be invoked to establish national programs in areas of exclusive provincial jurisdiction only with the approval of at least seven provinces representing 50 percent of the population. There would be reasonable compensation to non-participating provinces that establish their own programs meeting the objectives of the Canada-wide programs.

The federal government wishes to hold its residual power on national matters, but would give up the residual power over non-national matters not specifically mentioned in the constitution. The federal package suggests no changes with respect to the financing of social programs or to the system of equalization.

The most significant economic thrust in the federal package deals with the economic union. The "common market" clause (Section 121) is to be expanded, declaring that Canada is an economic union within which persons, goods, services and capital move freely without barriers or restrictions based on provincial or territorial boundaries. Neither Ottawa nor the provinces shall by law or practice contravene this principle, although exceptions are allowed for regional development programs and laws declared by Ottawa to be in the national interest. Furthermore, it is proposed that "the Parliament of Canada may exclusively make laws in relation to any matter that it declares to be for the efficient functioning of the economic union." Such laws would have no effect unless approved by at least seven provinces representing 50 percent of the population. Provinces may opt out of these laws for three years. And finally, the federal government proposes to develop, with the provinces, guidelines to improve coordination of fiscal policies and the harmonization of fiscal policies with Canada's monetary policy. Once approved, these guidelines would be adopted in federal legislation under the new economic union power, requiring approval of at least seven provinces representing 50 percent of the population.

Although not strictly a constitutional issue, the proposals recommend that the Bank of Canada's mandate be stated as "to achieve and preserve price stability" and that there be more regional representation in developing Bank policy.

A new national institution is proposed, the Council of the Federation, composed of federal, provincial and territorial governments that would meet on issues of intergovernmental coordination and collaboration. The Council would be the body for implementing the seven province-50 percent rule governing the federal spending power, laws under the economic union and guidelines for fiscal harmonization.

The federal document contains twenty-eight proposals,

creating a complex web, but it might be summarized with three themes.

- It attempts to accommodate several visions of Canada and therefore is not a strong assertion of Pan-Canadian ideals.
- There is little explicit decentralization, but a framework of great flexibility is recommended.
- There are explicit, detailed proposals to enhance the economic union using a new federal power and the Council of the Federation.

The Quebec Model

A federal structure, which accommodates Quebec's demands for increased powers while preserving the existing balance between Ottawa and the remainder of the provinces, might be called asymmetric federalism. Not surprisingly the most explicit model of asymmetric federalism has been proposed by Quebec, most recently in the Allaire Report — *A Québec Free to Choose*.

The Allaire Report proposes almost complete devolution of power to Quebec; indeed it speaks of political autonomy for Quebec. Quebec would "exercise exclusive discretionary and total authority in most fields of activity," and there would be a concomitant shift in taxing powers. Quebec would have full sovereignty in twenty-two areas and nine areas would be shared between Quebec and Canada. The central government would have exclusive authority only in defence, customs, currency and debt, and equalization. The size of the central government would of course be substantially reduced. The federal spending power would be eliminated. There is no mention of national social programs in the report; equalization would be retained.

There would be a complete restructuring of national institutions including abolition of the Senate as it exists. Decisions of Quebec courts could no longer be appealed to the Supreme Court of Canada. The nation, such as it remains, would be based on "the free and voluntary membership of participating states." There is no mention of the role of other provinces. Quebec is envisioned as a sovereign entity that would make a pact with the rest of Canada. How the rest of Canada chooses to organize itself is not at issue.

Perhaps surprisingly, the Allaire Report contains a vigorous defence of the Canadian economic and monetary union. It argues that there remain many restrictions on trade and mobility of resources, and that these should be removed. Furthermore, it calls for harmonization of tax and fiscal policies. The Report is silent on the administrative or political mechanism to maintain the economic and monetary union.

This extreme asymmetric federalism can also be summarized with three themes.

• There is no national vision, only a vision of a sovereign Quebec entering into arrangements with others.

• There are specific and detailed proposals for virtually complete decentralization.

• The economic and monetary union are to be enhanced, but there are no details about how.

The contrast with the federal proposals is sharp indeed. The federal government offers vagueness on division of powers and specifics on the economic union. Quebec offers specifics on the division of powers and vagueness on the economic union.

Quebec might be willing to accept a less severe form of asymmetry, but the alternative, at a minimum, would have to include the five conditions contained in the Meech Lake Accord and significant changes to the division of powers. Depending upon the degree of asymmetry, the role of Quebec representatives in national institutions would have to be reconsidered.

A Decentralized Federalism

A decentralized model arises in the belief that Canada is highly regionalized, with diverse tastes for government services. Those groups that favour decentralization believe that local government is better able to match government programs with local conditions. They believe decentralization is also desirable because it fosters diversity and innovation, and creates competition among governments that will lead to efficient provision of services. Most important, decentralization may be a means to accommodate Quebec while retaining the notion that all provinces are equal and all citizens have equal rights as individuals.

The Group of 22 were prominent men and women from business, universities and the public sector, who gathered together to discuss constitutional reform. In *Some Practical Suggestions for Canada*, they have set out one example of a decentralized federation. This model balances the dual loyalties of nation and province, but shifts much responsibility to the provinces. The Group argues that confusion in the roles of governments and in the minds of citizens is rampant. Although some constitutional reform is necessary, there is much to be gained by respecting the constitution we have. They would clarify the respective roles of the federal and provincial governments to ensure constitutional equality between the two layers of government. The Government of Canada would have particular responsibility in international relations, national security and management of the economy. Provincial governments would be responsible for the provision of most public services that touch citizens directly.

The Group of 22 recommends decentralization of social policy. Income security, including pensions, family benefits, welfare and income supplements, are local or regional in nature and should be devolved to the provinces. The income-supplement portion of unemployment insurance would be transferred to the provinces. The federal government should withdraw from its explicit financing of education and health. The federal government would transfer the fiscal resources it currently devotes to these programs, via tax room and a new general transfer payment, to the provinces. It would also revise the equalization formula so that poorer provinces would not suffer from the shift. The report includes a recommendation that national standards still be preserved, and that local decisions be harmonized to protect mobility, but includes no detail about how these could be achieved.

The report suggests that provinces have primary responsibility for culture. The Parliament of Canada would only retain a role with respect to cultural institutions and activities having a national and international dimension. The environment, transport, fisheries, energy and natural resources, regional development and job training would be provincial except insofar as there would be clear interprovincial issues or international issues. Regional economic development would be provincial. The federal spending power would be abolished as would the federal residual power.

The Group "recommend full and complete recognition of the four economic freedoms — the free movement of labour, capital, goods and services — be stipulated in the constitution so that the Canadian economic union can be fully established, and citizens can have recourse to the courts to ensure these provisions are met." An administrative tribunal would oversee the practical realization of these economic freedoms and assist in the resolution of problems. It also recommends "provincial governments commit themselves to a mandatory and independent review of their fiscal policies and plans, together with the federal government, and the release of an annual publication reporting on Canadian monetary and fiscal policies."

The Senate would be reformed and named the House of the Federation, to be elected or appointed by the provinces. It would review Commons' legislation in the area of federal-provincial relations, oversee national standards in appropriate areas of provincial policy and monitor the economic union tribunal.

This decentralized model may be summarized as expounding the following three themes.

• Canada is a federation of provinces, with a national government.

• The federal government is responsible for international issues and management of the economy; provincial governments are responsible for most public services.

• The economic union and national standards in social policy would be handled by administrative tribunals and a House of the Federation.

The Beaudoin-Dobbie Report

The 1991 federal proposals became the focus for discussion after their release, with the Quebec model, a decentralized federalism and a Pan-Canadian vision in the background as alternatives. Pressures continued for further movement on aboriginal self-government, a Triple-E Senate and the inclusion of a social charter. A Special Joint Committee of the Senate and the House of Commons was appointed, under the joint chair of Gérald Beaudoin (Senate) and Dorothy Dobbie (House of Commons), to provide Canadians an opportunity "to participate fully in the development of the government of

Canada's plan for a renewed Canada." The Committee held meetings across the country, heard from hundreds of individuals and received thousands of submissions. The Committee also participated in five constitutional conferences, organized by major research institutes and sponsored by the federal government, dealing with the division of powers, the reform of democratic institutions, the renewal of the economic union, and the shared rights and values of Canadians. These conferences were held in Halifax, Calgary, Montreal and Toronto. A concluding conference held in Vancouver reviewed the consensus developed at the first four.

The Beaudoin-Dobbie Report retained the basic framework of the federal proposals, attempting to accommodate several visions, but made changes, most notably articulating our shared national interests. It rejected a major break from our constitutional past, asserting the Canadian way is the path of gradualism, flexibility and liberty.

The Committee began by trying to identify our common interests, isolating three in particular: economic interests, social interests and cultural interests.

Our shared economic interests require that the economic union be preserved and enhanced. The common market clause (Section 121) would be replaced with a statement that "Canada is an economic union within which goods, services, persons and capital may move freely." Federal and provincial laws should not impede the efficient functioning of the economic union. Exceptions would be allowed, especially for equalization and regional development. The Committee preferred that the courts not be the forum for settling disputes; rather it suggested a tribunal of experts to review, conciliate and decide, should conciliation fail. The Committee would not grant the federal government a new head power over the economic union, nor create a Council of the Federation with a role in managing the union. There was no explicit discussion of how to coordinate federal and provincial fiscal policies, and the Committee recommended that changes to the Bank of Canada's mandate not be part of the constitutional discussions.

The Report argues that our network of social programs has become one of the strongest elements of our Canadian identity and should be recognized in a social covenant. Section 36 of the *Constitution Act, 1982* would be amended to commit jointly all levels of government to providing comprehensive universal health care; to providing adequate social services and benefits; to providing universal primary and secondary education and reasonable access to post-secondary education; to protecting the right to organize and bargain collectively; and to protecting the environment.

Section 36 would be extended to commit governments jointly to the economic union, free mobility of persons, goods, services and capital, the goal of full employment and ensuring all Canadians have a reasonable standard of living. Section 36 would therefore deal with both the social covenant and the economic union.

An inter-governmental review agency would be established to report on how governments are meeting the goals of the social covenant and the economic union. A conference of first ministers would meet annually "to discuss economic and social matters affecting Canada."

The constitutional arrangements for interests and values common to all Canadians currently include the *Canadian Charter of Rights and Freedoms* and mobility rights. The Committee would add commitments to the economic union and a social covenant. These common interests would be the responsibility of both federal and provincial governments. The Committee also notes, as have many others including the authors of the Allaire Report, that on fundamental values of a political culture there is a remarkable agreement across Canada.

The Committee also recognized "an increasingly impressive body of cultural achievements, creations and institutions" in Canada and argued the preservation and extension of this heritage must be pursued in the process of constitutional renewal. The Committee believes that a federal presence in culture is essential for the well-being and development of the cultural sector in Canada, for national unity and the survival of Canada as a nation.

The Committee calls the need to establish our common interests and values and give them constitutional form, the challenge of vision. The Committee then turns to our diversity, to the need for autonomy of provinces, regions, local and cultural communities. To give this constitutional form is called the challenge of inclusion. The special needs of Quebec, aboriginal peoples, of provinces outside central Canada, and the need to reflect the gender balance and diversity of Canadian society must be addressed. Our federal system strives to balance the needs of the national and provincial, of the general and the specific, of interdependence and autonomy.

This balance would be articulated in the new constitution in the preamble and the Canada clause. Quebec would be recognized as a distinct society. Canada's linguistic duality would be recognized. The inherent right of aboriginal peoples to self-government in Canada would be entrenched.

Balance would also be achieved via a reformed Senate that would be directly elected by proportional representation, with senators having fixed terms of no more than six years. Each province would not have an equal number of senators, but smaller provinces would have a greater share of senators than their population share. The powers of the Senate would be the same as those of the Commons, except on supply bills; in cases of deadlock on any bill, the Commons could override a Senate veto.

The Report also recommends that the appointment of judges to the Supreme Court would be from lists supplied by provincial and territorial governments and that there would be three from Quebec. Several amending formulae are proposed, and the Committee recommends Quebec have a veto over changes in federal institutions.

Like the federal proposals, the Beaudoin-Dobbie Report makes modest proposals for decentralization but recommends a framework of great flexibility. It rejects the idea that the two orders of government can operate in "water-tight compartments," instead arguing that we need arrangements for managing interdependence.

Immigration and agriculture are now concurrent powers, but federal law is paramount. The Committee would extend this approach to inland fisheries and personal bankruptcy. It recommends studies to eliminate unnecessary overlap and duplication in all areas of shared jurisdiction. It would allow legislative delegation, but only under very stringent conditions ensuring full public debate and participation. The Committee recommends that exclusive provincial jurisdiction in labour market training and culture be recognized, and acknowledges implicit or explicit provincial jurisdiction in tourism, forestry, mining, recreation, housing and municipal-urban affairs. Regional development, family policy and energy might be added to this list. In all of these areas the federal government also has a role, either under the spending power or under another related jurisdiction. The Committee recommends that the two levels of government negotiate agreements to clarify their roles and that such agreements could not be changed unilaterally. This proposal is a reaction to the federal government's expenditure control plan that unilaterally limited cash transfers under the Established Programs Financing Act and the Canada Assistance Plan. The federal spending power would be acknowledged, but a province could opt out with compensation if the province carries on a program that meets the objectives of the Canada-wide program.

The federal system in the Beaudoin-Dobbie Report may be summarized by referring to the three themes of unity, diversity and management of interdependence.

• A national vision is articulated, rooted in the economic union, the social covenant, and the Charter of Rights.

• Many jurisdictions are shared, but greater provincial autonomy can be obtained through intergovernmental agreement, opting out and legislative delegation.

• The economic union, social covenant and management of interdependence are shared responsibilities of federal, provincial and territorial governments.

Since the Beaudoin-Dobbie Report was released, representatives of the federal government, the provinces, the territories and aboriginal peoples have been meeting to develop further constitutional proposals. The proposals had not been released when this book went to press. No doubt further changes will be made before formal constitutional amendments are placed before the House of Commons, the Senate, and the legislative assemblies of the provinces. The final outcome, whatever it is, will be some mix of the four alternatives discussed above. Assessment of these alternatives will provide the building blocks necessary to evaluate any further alternative.

4

Economic Principles
and Constitutional Design

Can economic analysis help us to choose among the various alternative federal structures? Obviously economics cannot be the sole guide to constitutional design, nor perhaps even the main one, but economics cannot be ignored. Economic principles can assist in drafting the constitution: in deciding on the division of powers, the financing of social programs and role of the economic union.

A prescription for constitutional design using economic principles starts from a conception of the role of government in society, especially in economic affairs. These conceptions are fundamental values; some might call them ideologies. Roughly speaking, there are those who believe in a minimalist state, those who believe in a mixed economy, and those who believe in an activist state. These beliefs arise from an inseparable mix of value judgements, interpretations of history and ideas about human nature, not from economic principles.

Minimalists value liberty above all and would limit the role of government. They argue that most government actions, ostensibly pursuing the common good, are actually power-grabs by some interest group or other. Minimalist constitutions would grant governments few powers, limited mainly to providing a framework for civil society. They would emphasize small government units, competing against each other, in order to limit the scope for abuse of power. They might even require large majorities for the passage of laws and put restrictions on deficits and debt.

Mixed economy proponents try to strike a balance between public and private activity. They have an individualist perspective, judging society's well-being according to the aggregation of individual well-being in the belief that individuals are the best judge of what is good for them. But fairness is also valued. There is the possibility that redistribution could make society as a whole better off. A fundamental purpose of the political process under the constitution is to work out our ideas of fairness and to implement them through redistribution. Competitive private markets may be an efficient mechanism for the allocation of resources, but they can fail to achieve the most desirable outcomes. Government, as a fairly benevolent agent in society, has the role of correcting market failures while at the same time facilitating the operation of the private market. Constitutions recognize the government's role in stabilizing the economy, providing certain public services and social programs, redressing market failures and redistributing income.

Activists tend to be suspicious of the private market, emphasizing that the pursuit of individual interest seldom achieves our common interests. The government is the agent for the common interest: government represents the collectivity. This view often favours public or third-sector provision over private provision of services, and sees government playing a strategic, leadership role in social and economic affairs. Activists see our society as characterized by great inequality determined by income, race and gender. Government must intervene on behalf of the weak against the strong, and help alter society, eradicating these inequalities. Activist constitutions do not constrain governments and, because it is thought global economic forces threaten government social programs and commitments to redistribution, these constitutions would impose obligations on government to do certain things. A social charter is in the activist tradition, obliging government to provide certain social services.

With our usual penchant for compromise, Canada has chosen a middle road in the postwar period. Although we have proponents of both the minimalist and activist ideologies, government's actual role in the postwar period is consistent with a mixed economy view, the view which underlies the following discussion.

Division of Powers

Assuming we have sorted out the legitimate domain of government, the question arises: why not have a unitary system of government rather than a federal system? Should all powers be assigned to one level of government or should powers be divided between national and provincial levels and, if so, how should the division be made?

As a starting principle, economists tend to say a decentralized government is best, recommending against a unitary state. People's tastes vary across the country, and to ensure that governments provide the services people want, the government should be close to the people. Decentralized government will be more efficient and more accountable.

The essence of the argument is the variation in people's tastes. In larger jurisdictions, it is more likely that some citizens will want government to provide more public services and other citizens will want government to provide fewer public services. In larger jurisdictions, more people are dissatisfied with the level of service. With smaller jurisdictions, it is more probable that the actual services provided will match people's tastes. Assuming that tastes toward public services vary by province, this logic recommends substantial powers at the provincial level.

The presumption in favour of decentralization is an organizing principle of the European Community, and given the opaque label of "subsidiarity." But there is an important difference for Canada. In the European Community, the central authority has no independent sovereignty, only sovereignty granted by the member states. Subsidiarity is a principle to minimize the loss of sovereignty by member states. In Canada, the sovereignties of the national government and the provincial governments were created simultaneously.

Do tastes, in fact, vary by province? There is great similarity in the basic values of the political culture: equality, non-discrimination, representative democracy, the rule of law, belief in order and mutual help through social provision. We are probably more similar now than at any time in our history. Also most evidence suggests similar tastes for government expenditure, at least over large expenditure categories. There has been considerable similarity across provinces in the components, size and growth of expenditures. Alberta might favour an unemployment insurance scheme with more incentives to work; Quebec might favour user charges in health care; and Ontario might favour non-profit daycare over for-profit daycare. But these are matters of degree. It would seem tastes do not vary too much. A national program, allowing modest provincial variation, would seem to be consistent with the distribution of tastes. Just as a modest amount of provincial cooperation would produce a very similar system across the country.

Against the principle of decentralization, economics sets a number of other considerations. The benefits of government activities are not always confined to a local area. Some activities will benefit the entire country, regardless of who provides them. The textbook example is defence. If New Brunswick were to patrol the Atlantic coast, the sovereignty of the entire nation is defended. These national public services might better be the responsibility of the national government. And of course, constitutions almost always assign defence to the national government. As another example, some types of research benefit the entire country, and therefore assistance to research would be a national responsibility.

Economies of scale are another consideration. Just as some goods are more efficiently produced by small firms (for example, restaurant meals) and other goods are more efficiently produced by large firms (for example, automobiles), the same holds true for government goods and services. To illustrate this point with an example, in a large metropolitan area, it is more efficient to have one fire department with one dispatcher and one maintenance yard and one personnel office, than to have a separate fire department in each local municipality with several dispatchers, maintenance yards and personnel offices.

The empirical evidence on economies of scale is mixed, and of course the possibility for economies will differ by each public service. Services for which there are significant fixed costs — such as a system for processing insurance claims and mailing cheques — have economies of scale. But the assignment of powers to provinces remains problematic. If Quebec is the efficient size for providing a service, all the Maritime provinces are too small and a regional system would be needed. If New Brunswick is the efficient level for producing another service, then Ontario would require more than thirteen subjurisdictions.

Finally, externalities complicate the division of powers. The benefits, or costs, of one government's action often spill over into another's jurisdiction. If Ontario pays to reduce effluent flowing into Lake Ontario, Quebec, downstream on the St. Lawrence, will benefit. And of course the reverse is also true. If Ontario does not reduce its effluent, Quebec will suffer. Examples proliferate quickly. A person educated in Newfoundland may move to Alberta. Or provincial rent controls may force the federal government to assist rental housing. Or Quebec's sovereignist aspirations may increase its unemployment, while the rest of the nation shares the financial burden of unemployment insurance payments. Economic efficiency requires some mechanism so that all the affected people are involved in the decision. One such mechanism is to assign responsibility to a higher level of government. Another is to allow provincial control and establish institutional and legal arrangements to negotiate assigning the external costs and benefits.

Equalization and Social Programs
Since the middle of the twentieth century, the bulk of government spending has been in the areas of health, education, income assistance and other forms of social protection. Many Canadians believe that certain minimum standards of living and social protection are the right of every Canadian citizen. Such rights are clear in the United Nations' Universal Declaration of Human Rights, which Canada has signed. Article 25 of the Declaration states "Everyone has the right to a standard of living adequate for the health and well-being of himself and of his family, including food, clothing, housing and medical care and necessary social services, and the right to security in the event of unemployment, sickness and disability, widowhood, old age or other loss of livelihood in circumstances beyond his control." Let us call these "the rights of citizenship." Perhaps the national government should be responsible for such rights to ensure they are equally available, just as all citizens have the right to vote and the right to equal treatment before the law. (Similar sentiments also demand rights contained in the *Canadian Charter of*

Rights and Freedoms apply equally to all citizens across the country.)

Of course, many other Canadians — notably Québécois and aboriginal peoples — reject this homogeneous notion of citizenship rights. Some of them want a separate nation altogether. Others struggle to create new concepts of citizenship in several communities within one country.

The "citizenship rights" to an adequate standard of living, education, health and security are expensive and necessarily involve a substantial amount of redistribution — from rich to poor, from healthy to sick, from one community to another. How these government responsibilities are assigned and financed will determine the spatial boundaries of our sharing community. Do we wish to have a linked system of sharing communities or do we want a national sharing community?

Typically, economists recommend that responsibility for redistribution be assigned to the highest level of government. If it were assigned to lower levels and this resulted in different levels of redistribution across the nation, people and firms would tend to move. People seeking benefits would move to the more generous jurisdiction, and other people and firms would move out of the high-tax jurisdiction. Local jurisdictions, hoping to attract desirable people or firms, might pursue beggar-thy-neighbour policies. With decentralized responsibility, we might end up with less redistribution than we would if we all sat down together.

Taxation

Given the division of expenditure and regulatory powers, tax levying powers need to be assigned. One approach is to decide independently on expenditure and taxing authority. Any imbalance between expenditures and revenues at any level of government could be redressed through intergovernmental grants. An alternative approach is to match expenditure responsibility with taxation responsibility, the theory being that the government that spends the money should have to confront taxpayers to raise it. And vice versa, the government that has raised the money should be ultimately responsible for how it is spent.

If tax authority is to be assigned independently, the principles of division are similar to those used for expenditure division. There are considerable economies of scale in tax design, operation and collection that call for centralization. Also if tax collection is decentralized and governments pursue uncoordinated tax policies, there can be fiscal externalities from one jurisdiction to another. For example, a province could tax the activities of nonresidents inside its borders and so export the tax burden. If one province were to tax an activity especially heavily, the activity might move elsewhere creating a larger tax base for its new location. Uncoordinated provincial tax policies can lead to too much or too little tax revenue.

Tax systems are not merely a means of financing expenditures. They are policy instruments themselves. The tax system is probably the most important government instrument for redistribution. It alters the distribution of income and wealth between rich and poor (vertical equity) and insures that individuals in similar circumstances are treated similarly (horizontal equity). If our vision of Canada stresses loyalty to the nation, we would define our ideas of equity at the national level. Vertical equity would imply a national tax system, or at least provincial systems with strong coordination, because if provinces pursued their own ideas of fairness they would violate national standards. Similarly, a national or highly coordinated system is required for horizontal equity to ensure that Canadian citizens, regardless of the province in which they live, are treated in a similar manner.

If our vision of Canada emphasizes provincial sovereignty in the larger whole, ideas of fairness would be established at the provincial level and could vary across provinces. Horizontal equity would only apply within provinces and not across provinces. Tax systems would then be provincially based and vary across provinces.

Tax provisions can be substitutes for direct expenditures. For example pollution control can be achieved through direct grants or through special tax deductibility of pollution-reducing investments (or through regulation). Tax systems can also be used in conjunction with expenditures. For example, the tax structure, job training and welfare payments together form an income-security system. If the federal or provincial governments had expenditure responsibilities for the environment or income security, there would be a need to assign them the complementary tax instruments.

Stabilization and Economic Union

The joint presentation of taxes and expenditures in a budget is the means of fiscal policy. If the management of fiscal policy is a national responsibility, as it is in most federations, there is a considerable centralization of both taxation and expenditure responsibilities.

However, other factors may recommend decentralization of taxation and expenditure, in which case the combined budgets of provincial governments can be larger than the national budget. Coordination of provincial budgets will be required to conduct a national fiscal policy. As Europe moves closer to an economic and monetary union, the need to coordinate national fiscal policies is emerging as an important issue.

Almost all countries share a single currency and therefore are a monetary union. Most economists would recommend that monetary policy be conducted by an independent central bank, outside the political system. Connections between the central bank and either the national or provincial governments would be desirable only to facilitate the exchange of information and to help legitimize the bank's policies.

If we stop to think about it, one primary reason for the existence of most federal states is the creation and maintenance of an economic union. This requires considerable homogeneity of expenditure programs, tax systems and coordination of fiscal policies in order to preserve the free movement of goods, capital, services and people. There must either be a strong central government or a means of forcing provincial harmonization.

To sum up, the application of economic principles to constitutional design usually assigns redistributive and stabilization functions to the nation. Spending powers are usually assigned to the provinces, except where the benefits are evidently national, where there are significant cross-provincial externalities and where there are large economies of scale. These require either national powers or interprovincial coordination. Maintenance of the economic union also requires national powers or strong harmonization and coordination. Although not without critics and counter views, these are the standard prescriptions of economics.

Do the Alternatives Reflect Economic Principles? Paper *

We have before us proposals for several alternative constitutional structures: the federal, Allaire Report, Group of 22 and Beaudoin-Dobbie models. Is any one of them more soundly based on economic analysis?

Perhaps it might be useful to begin with the division of powers and the areas where all the alternatives are in agreement. All would leave defence, customs and tariffs, currency and debt, and equalization at the national level. The first three are self-evidently of national implication. The fourth acknowledges that there is a national dimension of fairness to be addressed via interprovincial equalization and that the gains from economic union should be shared. From an economic point of view, these divisions make good sense.

Similarly, all would assign exclusively to the provincial level responsibility for tourism, forestry, mining, job training, recreation, housing, and municipal-urban affairs. These divisions do not appear to emerge entirely from economic logic. Recreation, housing, and municipal-urban affairs are functions of local influence for which there may be diversity of tastes across the nation. Housing policy, however, has always been a component of our national social safety net, and if housing assistance is not portable, it can reduce labour mobility within the economic union. Also, if an important determinant of the urban condition in one city is the evolution of the national system of cities, or if national prosperity depends upon how our cities link into the international system of cities, a national presence in an apparently local situation might be necessary.

Assignment to the provinces of mining and forestry is motivated more by a desire, rooted in our history, to have unambiguous provincial responsibility for natural resources than by economic analysis. Job training and tourism do have many local aspects, but they have just as many externalities, national aspects and international aspects. Economic principles would not recommend exclusive provincial responsibility in these areas.

Sometimes economic analysis of the division of powers runs counter to the existing constitution. For example, we might conclude that Ontario is too big for most functions and Prince Edward Island too small. Their boundaries were created at a time when the scope of government activity was limited and communication between regions was difficult and costly. Perhaps provincial boundaries should now be changed. Education is another controversial area. It generates substantial national externalities, so perhaps education should be a national responsibility even though it is unambiguously a provincial responsibility in our current constitution. Needless to say, none of the constitutional proposals considers a change in provincial boundaries or a reduction in existing provincial power.

Economic principles identify a few obvious federal responsibilities and a few obvious provincial responsibilities. Common sense dictates similar recommendations and not surprisingly, most constitutional proposals agree on these. But after this easy start, economic principles generate complexity and suggest functions must be analysed on a case-by-case basis. It also becomes evident that it is impossible to divide powers into watertight compartments. Suppose, for example, the federal government were assigned the responsibility for national defence and international trade, and so reasonably might be in charge of Halifax harbour. But Halifax harbour is part of the regional watershed and ecosystem, so a provincial responsibility in these regional matters will involve the harbour. And of course municipal politicians from neighbourhoods surrounding the harbour will want to influence harbour development. Management of the St. Lawrence and Great Lakes waterways raise similar issues. Even when a relatively clear division of powers is possible, there is interdependence and a need for coordination between governments.

But the issue is even deeper. Analysis of almost any policy problem — whether it is the environment, unemployment or child poverty — soon shows how multifaceted are the causes, how many existing government activities influence the problem, and how potentially multifaceted is further government policy. After any constitution is chosen, there will have to emerge a complex set of administrative arrangements and these will be constantly changing. Such arrangements are costly and time consuming to execute. We have these under our existing constitution, but they would have to be renegotiated if there were any major reallocation of powers.

One of the strongest arguments for decentralization is that there is now substantial and unnecessary overlap between the federal and provincial governments. The federal government is too involved in areas of provincial jurisdiction. This overlap means costly duplication — the proverbial eleven civil servants all doing the same job. It also means levels of government compete for the support of voters and offer programs in the same area: We get two programs where one would do.

In the abstract, the argument is appealing, but there is scant empirical evidence to prove either charge. There are strong arguments why the federal government might be involved in provincial matters. For example, in order to stabilize the economy and to provide equalization, the federal government might have to raise the bulk of the revenue although much of it then flows in transfers to the provinces. Basic democratic principles and recognition of national citizenship rights would require that the federal government take some responsibility for how the money is spent. So duplication does exist, but it is inevitable. Furthermore it is very hard to calculate how much of Ottawa's activity is coordination and would simply have to be undertaken by someone else in a more decentralized federation.

The alternative constitutional structures each offer a change in the division of powers. The main differences between them concern the extent of decentralization proposed. The Allaire Report and the Group of 22 recommend a major decentralization of the federation; the federal and Beaudoin-Dobbie proposals are much more modest. The former alternatives would eliminate the federal spending power; the latter would include it, with the possibility of opting out, in a new constitution. None, however, has set out the economic logic behind its recommendations. There is a strong but unsubstantiated presumption that tastes and conditions vary by province and, therefore, that provincial responsibility would yield better policy. There is scant discussion of economies of scale or of externalities, nor is there a measure of the current costs of duplication and coordination or of the administrative costs of alternative government structures. We are as likely to get more costly and less efficient government programs under any one of the proposals as we are to get cheaper and more efficient government.

Much of government expenditure is on social programs and social insurance, which are motivated mostly by equity concerns. The economic logic that assigns responsibility for redistribution to the national level presupposes that there is a national consensus on the degree of redistribution desirable and that access to social programs is a right of citizenship. The assignment of social policy in a constitution will change if there are different provincially-held attitudes to redistribution and if there is less emphasis on national citizenship rights. Economic analysis cannot recommend one of these value systems over another. The choice must be made on other grounds. However, economic analysis does point out that decentralized redistribution can have effects on mobility and can create intergovernmental competition that limits the level of social services. None of the constitutional proposals adequately discusses these issues.

Although the constitutional alternatives differ greatly on the division of powers and redistribution, there is a startling consensus on the desirability of an economic and monetary union. All contain ringing endorsements of the need to ensure the mobility of goods, services, capital and people, to break down barriers to this mobility and to have common business framework laws. All agree that there are gains from economic integration and that a federal nation should also be an economic and monetary union. Never before in our constitutional discussions has this economic logic been so forcefully stated.

Canada obviously has a monetary union and, by many standards, a very thoroughgoing economic union. There are perhaps more barriers in Canada than in some other federations, such as the United States, but our economic union is more complete than Europe will achieve by 1992. Significant barriers still remain to a complete union, caused both by the provincial and federal governments. However, their complete removal is not realistic and the additional gains in income from further integration would be modest. It is not the promise of additional gains that has brought attention to the economic union, but fear that the economic union will be fragmented as the nation decentralizes.

Although all the alternatives argue for an economic and monetary union, they differ on the details of how the economic union would be maintained. Under the federal proposals, the federal government would make laws for the economic union, but the laws would have to be approved by the Council of the Federation. Most provinces have expressed reservations about these proposals, but they have not offered alternatives.

Quebec has been conspicuously silent on proposing alternatives. This is a glaring gap. It ignores a basic contradiction; namely, that decentralization of powers allows more provincial autonomy and diversity, but economic integration means a loss of provincial sovereignty and a degree of economic, social and political harmonization. Also there is a risk that the economic union will fragment and the economy will balkanize following significant decentralization. This would make everyone worse off. Asymmetric or decentralist constitutional proposals are incomplete without a specification of how the economic union would be maintained and without a clear statement of the degree of economic and social harmonization envisaged.

There are several ways to sustain the economic union in a federal system. One way is through a strong central government with responsibility for the union. Another way is to create a forum through which the provinces would negotiate an economic union, define a subsidy code and establish a dispute settlement mechanism. Or, the responsibility can be shared between levels. All the proposals, except the Quebec model, are a hybrid of these three approaches. Another method is to establish the economic union in the constitution and let the courts decide if federal or provincial laws contravene the commitment to an economic union.

The economic literature on federalism usually assumes that fiscal policy is a major responsibility of government and assigns it to the national level. Provincial economies are too small and interconnected with economies beyond their borders to allow an independent fiscal policy. Curiously, none of the constitutional proposals discusses this responsibility directly. This partly reflects the current federal fiscal crisis: the commitment to controlling the deficit is so overriding that no new fiscal initiatives are possible to combat the recession. The efficacy of fiscal policy is under attack more generally from certain schools of economic thought, but the constitution should be not designed around a current fiscal stance or school of thought. Any significant shift of powers and revenues to the provinces will make federal fiscal policy more difficult. The combined budgets of the provinces, compared to the federal budget, would be even larger than they are now. Indeed the combined budgets of the bigger provinces would be larger. Therefore national fiscal policy could only be conducted by coordinating and harmonizing provincial fiscal policies. Both Allaire and the Group of 22 recognize this and make references to how it might be achieved. The federal proposals are more explicit. They suggest a relatively fixed budget cycle, a fixed annual schedule of finance ministers' meetings, common accounting conventions and budget guidelines set in federal law under the new economic union power but approved by the Council of the Federation. Not surprisingly the provinces have vigorously rejected this proposal. But again a paradox is evident. The redistribution of powers can so weaken the centre that a new centre must be recreated to coordinate the provinces. Provincial sovereignty must again be shared. The Beaudoin-Dobbie Report ignores the need for fiscal policy coordination.

Economics recommends that monetary policy be conducted by an independent central bank under a mandate from elected government. The Group of 22 and the federal proposals suggest a "price stability" mandate; Allaire does not mention the mandate and Beaudoin-Dobbie says it should not be part of current discussions. All the proposals call for more regional or provincial input into bank policy. But the implications of this are unclear because the bank pursues its given mandate with independence.

National Power or Provincial Coordination?

A subtle reading of the economic analysis of constitutional design reveals that, in principle, most functions could be assigned to any level of government. For example, national defence could be a provincial responsibility — the provinces would simply have to agree among themselves how much to contribute to a shared defence effort. If some function had substantial economies of scale, it could still be a provincial responsibility. Each province would simply buy the amount it desired from a centralized production facility. Or a national government could be responsible for even the most local of activities, even, for example, city parks. The national government would identify local preferences and deliver different sorts of parks in each community.

The choice between different federal structures ultimately rests on the difference in organizational costs, comprehensively defined, of running the government institutions needed to carry out a policy authorized in an expenditure area. These costs include not only setting up different levels of government and running them, but also the costs of intergovernmental coordination. Furthermore, citizens bear costs in order to make their views known to government. A centralized federation has low coordination costs; a decentralized federation has high costs of intergovernment collaboration and bargaining.

There are also important differences in the role of the political process, the courts and administrative tribunals under different federal structures. With a more centralized federation, political responsibility on national issues is more visible. The tradeoffs and coordination take place within national political parties and in the national Parliament. A decentralized federation in which national issues are handled with interprovincial agreements blurs political responsibility. Intergovernmental meetings offer apparently bland communiqués, but the nuance of the chosen words sends signals to those in the know. Citizens and interest groups have trouble penetrating the process and getting their concerns on the negotiating table. In an extremely decentralized model, the role of the courts, administrative tribunals and dispute settlement mechanisms would increase. The "national institutions" would become more like meetings of G-7 countries or international trade tribunals, and less like a national political system. In the European Community, there is growing concern about the lack of democratic accountability of its powerful coordinating institutions.

None of the constitutional proposals adequately addresses these organizational costs. The federal proposals create a new national institution, the Council of the Federation, which no doubt would soon require its own secretariat. The Group of 22 and Allaire proposals contain no estimate of the costs of achieving the desired level of coordination in economic and social policy. International experience suggests these costs would be high and that too little coordination would occur. The decentralized parts would begin to fragment. But then ironically, if Canada were to follow the current international trend, the parts would seek mechanisms to bring themselves together again. We would reestablish national authority.

5

Can the Alternatives Help Meet Our Economic Challenges?

Canada faces pressing economic challenges: a fiscal crisis, threats to its prosperity from declining productivity and globalization, and difficulties sustaining its health, education and income security programs. Constitutional stability is a precondition to meeting the challenges. Only then can politicians and citizens focus their attention. Perhaps one of the alternatives could even enhance our economic prospects.

The Fiscal Crisis

There can be little doubt that part of the current disenchantment with our national government is because of federal economic mismanagement. The recent critique from Quebec has voiced this and argued that the only solution is a substantial devolution of power to Quebec. A similar view is implicit in the push for general decentralization. Yet none of the renewed federalisms under discussion has any proposals to deal with the accumulated debt — they pretend we are designing a country from scratch. The fiscal crisis is ignored. Indeed devolution to Quebec or general decentralization can be seen as an attempt by the provinces to escape involvement with the federal debt problem. Both the Allaire and the Group of 22 proposals presume that devolution would be accompanied by enough funds from Ottawa to run the programs at their current levels. Quebec assumes the federal government would lower its tax rates, allowing Quebec room to raise its

tax rates. One estimate of a generalized Allaire decentralization implies that Ottawa would transfer all sales and excise
taxes to the provinces and retain only 50 percent of personal
income tax collections, instead of 61 percent. The Group of 22
presumes Ottawa would use a combination of tax room and a
new general-purpose transfer. Proper disentanglement
would require the tax-room strategy.

Whatever the means chosen, there would be a huge revenue transfer to the provinces. Ottawa currently spends over
$35 billion on transfers to persons through programs including
family allowances, unemployment insurance and old age pensions. The Allaire Report, if extended to all provinces, would
leave this at about $2 billion, while the Group of 22 would leave
this at about $11 billion. The existing transfers to the provinces
for health, education and welfare would be similarly reduced.
As Ottawa's responsibilities were reduced, it would need fewer
civil servants and fewer buildings, but the provincial capitals
would require more civil servants and more buildings. This
would also require a revenue transfer from Ottawa to the prov-

Federal Spending Under Alternative Federal Structures ($ billions)			
	1991 Federal Budget	Generalized Allaire	Group of 22
Transfers to People	35.8	1.7	10.7
Transfers to Provinces	23.3	9.0	9.0
Other Transfers	11.6	2.5	4.0
Ottawa's Operating Costs	18.0	12.0	14.0
Payments to Crown Corporations	4.9	4.9	4.9
Defence	12.1	12.1	12.1
Foreign Aid	2.6	2.6	2.6
Public Debt Charges	43.0	43.0	43.0
Total	151.3	87.8	100.3

Source: 1991 Federal Budget and Toronto Star Calculations,
Toronto Star, September 22, 1991

inces. In all, a generalized Allaire approach would cut Ottawa's program spending by almost 60 percent, while the Group of 22 would cut it by almost 50 percent.

But after this devolution, Ottawa would have the same massive debt that it has today and the same annual deficit. Borrowings would be over 30 percent of its annual total expenditure, instead of 20 percent today. Interest charges would be 50 percent of annual expenditures under a generalized Allaire, compared to 28 percent today. If Ottawa is now tottering under its fiscal burdens, it would collapse with significant devolution.

The fiscal crisis is a national problem that requires a national solution. The current constitutional reform packages that call for decentralization with full financial compensation can only make the federal crisis worse. A reasonable quid pro quo for giving a province responsibility for an expenditure area would be to give it responsibility also for that portion of the national debt associated with the expenditure area. For ease of illustration, assume that two thirds of the national debt or $300 billion was associated with program spending (the rest was to finance the acquisition of assets). If decentralization were to reduce federal program spending by 50 percent, then the provinces would have to take on responsibility for $150 billion in debt. Most provinces could not take on this burden immediately — they could not go to the capital markets and borrow such sums. The transfer of debt responsibility would have to be more gradual. One means of gradual transfer would be to leave Ottawa responsible for the debt, but give the provinces less tax room to recognize Ottawa's debt burden, or to not provide a fully compensating cash transfer to the provinces. But this is just what Ottawa has been doing under its expenditure control plan — although only in the most modest way — to howls of protest. Decentralization would accelerate this process, if proper attention were paid to the debt.

We are not designing a constitution for a new country; we have a history, and part of that history is the accumulated federal debt associated with federal expenditure responsibilities — both its exclusive responsibilities and its participation in provincial responsibilities under the spending power. We must evaluate each constitutional proposal to see if it will help to deal with the fiscal crisis. It is hard to see how any of the constitutional reform proposals mentioned would help Canada deal with the fiscal crisis, and they could make a bad situation worse.

Suppose Ottawa were left with all the debt, as existing proposals seem to suggest. Ottawa would be taxing citizens and using much of the money to pay interest on the debt; but it would have little contact with citizens because it would not share in providing the services that affect our lives. Ottawa's main responsibilities would be defence and foreign affairs — important fields but far removed from daily life. Ottawa's taxes would be more and more resented; resistance to tax increases might be greater. The deficit and debt might increase.

If the provinces did take a share of the debt burden, and so a share of the need for fiscal restraint, Ottawa's burden would be reduced but our collective task might still be harder. Each provincial economy is smaller and less diversified than the national economy. Capital markets require higher interest rates on provincial borrowings. In partitioning up the restraint burden we can no longer use the diversified national economy, with its mutual insurance aspects, as an advantage in dealing with the debt burden.

Some people have argued that we have a national debt problem because of our federal structure. They argue that there has been wasteful duplication in that Ottawa's continual juggling of regional demands has led it to overspend. They would also claim that because Ottawa shares the cost, the provinces have not limited their expenditures or designed programs with an eye to restraint. Furthermore the shared federal-provincial responsibility has meant intergovernmental political competition and extra expenditures; and the murky responsibility in our federal-provincial system has placed few restraints on expansionist government bureaucracies. Each of these arguments may have some merit, although empirical evidence to support them is limited. Decentralization with a share of the debt burden might make fiscal restraint easier. But the arguments should not be used to justify wholesale constitutional change without assessing how the *new* system will deal with *existing* debt. This assessment has been lacking so far.

Our Threatened Prosperity

Quebec's current demands for greater powers have a different basis than in the past. Extra powers are needed not just to preserve and promote its distinctive language and culture; extra powers are needed also to pursue its economic objectives. Federalism no longer works economically, it is claimed, and a more independent Quebec would be better able to secure its economic prosperity.

Quebec does not discuss an economic strategy for Canada, but presumably what works for Quebec would work for other regions and therefore a generalized argument would conclude that Canada's future prosperity requires significant decentralization. The Group of 22 does not advance this argument. It would have the federal government primarily responsible for managing the economy although decentralizing social policy. The federal proposals say economic security rests on preserving and enhancing the economic union.

The Allaire Report declares "throughout the Western world, the role of the state is changing, but Canada seems quite unable to follow suit. It seems to be increasingly cut off from the new international and political realities." Furthermore, "constant language and cultural conflicts are now magnified by a financial and economic crisis without precedent in the history of Canadian federalism. Structural problems sap the economy and go unresolved for lack of consensus among the country's provinces and regions. It is becoming increasingly obvious that the Canadian federal state is based on centralizing practices dictated by an inflexible will to standardize public services to the utmost and the pursuit of grand so-called 'national policies.' But these federal concerns are poorly suited to the real needs of the provinces, businesses and people."

The Allaire Report sketches the economic strategy Quebec would pursue to meet the challenge of declining productivity and globalization. There would be a slight reduction in the role of the state, following the worldwide neo-conservative trend. But the state would remain a catalyst of economic development, creating institutions and financing infrastructure to support economic growth. Quebec has considerable experience in state-assisted capitalism under what has become known as "Quebec, Inc.": Hydro-Québec, the Caisse de dépôts, the Société générale de financement and so on. The Report proclaims there exists "a Quebec development model, along with Japanese and German. This model is the culmination of thirty years of economic nationalism" and is underpinned by a consensus among the political class, the labour movement and the business community. All this is to be conducted in the Canadian economic union and the vast North American free trade area.

Quebec evidently has an economic strategy that it wants to pursue, and one that commands considerable consensus within the province. Quebec is also ahead of the rest of Canada in recognizing the changing economic landscape; probably because, with one eye always cocked toward independence, it has been thinking for years about a strategy for economic security. Quebec more than anyone in the constitutional debate is arguing economic prosperity requires constitutional change.

Without debating the merits of Quebec's economic strategy, there are a number of questions. As mentioned, substantial decentralization must also recognize extra responsibility for the national debt. This has not been acknowledged in the Allaire proposals. More critically the Allaire proposals seek economic and political sovereignty in a Canadian economic union and a North American free trade area. But this is a fundamental contradiction. The extra economic sovereignty is required for a more complete pursuit of Quebec, Inc., a strategy different from other regions of the country. This significant difference, however, is inconsistent with participation in an economic union. An economic union requires a loss of economic sovereignty: reduced barriers to mobility, less regional economic nationalism, common business framework laws and harmonized tax and fiscal policies. The contradiction has been painfully exposed by the federal proposals for an economic union.

It is unclear how widely recognized this contradiction is in Quebec; given the sophistication of its economic strategists, the contradiction is likely recognized. Participation in the Canadian economic union demands some loss of sovereignty to an authority outside Quebec. The nub is the form of this outside authority. The Allaire model would totally restructure our central institutions to create a Quebec-Canada federation. Representatives from Quebec and representatives from Canada would manage the economic union. Quebec would begin from total sovereignty and only release it through negotiation; the central authority would have no independent sovereignty. The Quebec-Canada structure would be analogous to the European Community's management of their common market. Quebec would be a nation state within a federation of two. This is Quebec's preferred option, but it is likely unacceptable to the rest of Canada. If the Quebec model were generalized to all provinces, the economic union would be managed by ten sovereign provinces. This is the ultimate realization of the vision of Canada as a pact among provinces, and again the central authority has no independent sovereignty. Under a Pan-Canadian vision, the Government of Canada has independent sovereignty. The national Parliament, composed of representatives from all parts of the country, is the forum to manage issues which transcend provincial boundaries. The national government would be responsible for the economic union. The current Quebec mood finds this the least acceptable option for authority outside Quebec. The current federal proposals have a foot in both camps: the national government could make laws for the economic union, but initiatives would have to be approved by seven provinces representing 50 percent of the population in the Council of the Federation. The Group of 22 would make management of the economy primarily a federal responsibility; the Beaudoin-Dobbie Report emphasizes shared responsibility.

Quebec would gain some small extra amount of economic sovereignty under the Allaire model of decentralization with an economic union (but would gain a vital symbolic change in the nature of central authority). If wisely used, the sovereignty might enhance Quebec's prosperity. Also there would perhaps be some savings by reducing government overlap, although Quebec would face some offsetting increased coordination costs. There may be more efficient government programs because of greater clarity of responsibility. And maybe Quebec could make the tough economic decisions, that Canada seems unable to reach, because Quebec is a more cohesive society. But there are risks as well. The economic union might fragment, causing losses to Quebec which overwhelm any gains.

If the Allaire model has not sorted out what forum of central authority it would accept and what type of harmonization will be required, the other proposals have similar blank spots. The Group of 22 would have the federal government manage the economy and decentralize social policy. But it is unclear how the federal government could conduct a fiscal policy when most of the expenditure is at the provincial level. Also, many people believe that closer integration of economic and social policy is critical to economic adjustment. For example, unemployment insurance and welfare need to have more work incentives, and education will be a vital part of an economic strategy. Separating responsibility for economic and social policy will make integration more difficult. And other critics have claimed that regions have become dependent on federal transfers and are diverted from making the adjustments necessary for economic vitality and self reliance. A fundamental rethinking of our equalization system will be needed. This is postponed by the decentralist proposals, which place great emphasis on retaining existing equalization systems.

The federal proposals emphasize enhancing the economic union as the key to prosperity. They are correct in that a fragmented union would be costly. But they are wrong in implying there are substantial further gains to be had. Our economic union is quite complete and the feasible further reduction of barriers and further harmonization are modest. Beyond this, the proposals support no implicit or explicit economic strategy.The strong economic union proposals do, however, stand as a necessary counterweight to decentralization, if it were to occur.

The Beaudoin-Dobbie Report contains the least discussion of economic issues. The provisions for the economic union are much less precise and comprehensive than the federal proposals and there is no analysis of whether the proposed constitutional structure would lead to better economic policy.

While Quebec has declared the economic strategy it wishes to follow, the rest of Canada has not. There is no consensus. One school has emphasized deficit reduction, with fiscally driven decentralization, and a reduced role of government, freer trade and stable prices. These provide the framework for creating market-based prosperity. Another school rejects free trade and government withdrawal, favouring a more European-style social-democratic model. Still another argues that the system of regional redistribution has created transfer dependency in the regions. Only by weaning regions off transfers can economic vitality be secured. However, even within each school there is disagreement about what constitutional structure is required to implement the program. Indeed it can be argued that if a consensus existed on any economic strategy it could be implemented by any constitutional structure.

Much of our constitutional jockeying is really jockeying about economic strategy. If we like what the federal government is currently doing, we favour a strong central government. If we like what our provincial government is doing, we favour stronger provincial governments. But this is controversy about policy and does not belong in a debate about a constitution. Probably the only hypothesis that could have relevance is that the balance of political forces in the existing Canadian federation has prevented Canada from confronting its economic challenges and from making adjustments. Under this hypothesis, devolution of power would alter the political forces and permit better economic policy. There is no strong evidence to substantiate the hypothesis, so it remains a hypothesis not a conclusion, and a vague and speculative one at that.

One should not overstate the controversy surrounding economic renewal — consensus exists on certain items. Almost everyone agrees that maintaining the economic union is necessary and somewhat freer trade is inevitable. Also there is agreement that greater emphasis on education and public infrastructure is needed. But again, it is uncertain whether constitutional change is needed to go in these directions.

And finally, we can all agree that our constitutional problems have diverted governments' attention from our economic problems. Canada has painful economic adjustments to make and needs a fundamental rethinking of its economic strategy in the era of globalization. Constitutional stability is a most important step toward future prosperity, and probably a necessary precondition.

The Future of Social Programs

Social programs are discussed in considerable detail in the constitutional proposals. The Group of 22 and the Allaire Report would assign them exclusively to the provinces, with accompanying federal transfers or tax adjustments to finance them. The federal proposals would retain the current arrangements. The Beaudoin-Dobbie Report recommends that there be a social covenant committing governments to social programs and that there be no unilateral changes to the federal-provincial financing of social programs.But all of the discussion is about who shall be in charge, not about how the programs can be sustained. In their own way, all the proposals are oriented to the status quo. Canadians are worried about the future of social programs, and with good reason, but the constitutional changes do not address the need for a fundamental rethinking.

After the last several federal budgets, the system we have used to finance social programs is in disarray. Many of our social programs, in health, education, and income security, fall under provincial jurisdiction but have been converted into national programs using the federal spending power and intergovernmental grants. There was a substantial national commitment to these programs. However, recent federal budgets have put limits on the growth of federal transfers. The federal commitment seems to be eroding rapidly. Some critics worry that explicit federal transfers to provinces will end. The only federal support would be the tax room transferred years ago, which provides no leverage to ensure national standards. Our social policy framework is being transformed without debate. Federal decisions that affect social programs were made unilaterally and were driven by a desire to reduce the federal deficit, not by a desire to reform our system of financing social programs.

Proposals to decentralize authority to the provinces, with some adjustment to share the debt burden, would accelerate this process of federal withdrawal. Federal commitment retreats just as pressure on social programs builds from the fiscal crisis and industrial readjustment.

One way to resist these changes is through constitutional reform, most directly through a social charter. Proponents of a social charter see a constitution as more than a framework for civil society, setting out the rights of citizens and defining a clearly circumscribed domain of government. To them a constitution is also a statement of society's values, it is a form of social contract between citizens and government. Such a constitution not only places limits on government action but places obligations on governments. A social charter might oblige government to provide education, health care and income security for all. A charter could place obligations on both federal and provincial governments, and thus restrain the current federal retreat. Some advocates of a social charter see it as a means not only of retaining our existing social programs but also of extending them; the charter might, for example, oblige government to ensure all citizens had adequate food, clothing and shelter.

We already have an expression of social principles in our constitution, in Section 36 of the *Constitution Act, 1982.* It states that the Government of Canada and the provincial governments are committed to promoting equal opportunities and providing essential public services of reasonable quality to all Canadians. If a national government had an expansionary social agenda, this surely could provide constitutional justification. But the language is not strong enough to compel federal action.

This reveals a contentious feature of a social charter: it would specify government policy. It does not simply specify the rules of the game, it specifies the play of the game. A social charter that could bind governments would be a dramatic change in our democratic system. If the courts were to enforce a charter, the power over social policy would be outside Parliament. And social programs are always very costly, so Parliament would lose the power of the purse, perhaps its most fundamental power. By careful choice of constitutional language and design of enforcement mechanisms, the loss of parliamentary power could be mitigated. But fundamental issues remain that must be aired and carefully considered. Perhaps a social charter will be acknowledged as a momentous change in our system of government but on balance a desirable one; just as the *Canadian Charter of Rights and Freedoms* was a momentous change, but is now accepted by most Canadians as a desirable change.

There can be little doubt that some of the controversy

around a social charter is really a political debate about desirable policies. Some people want to sustain and expand social programs; others want to retrench. The proponents of retrenchment are currently winning in the political arena. So the proponents of expansion hope to win in the constitutional arena what they have been losing in the political. Here the critics of a charter dismiss it saying political forces must decide policy questions. But this logic is not being applied everywhere, and in any event, we must recognize that constitutions do constrain policy outcomes. For example, the mobility rights in an economic union constrain provincial industrial policies. Indeed some critics of the economic union proposals see them as a means to entrench a free-trade, free-market ideology in the constitution. They claim that opponents of many provincial laws, having lost in the political arena, are now trying to win in the constitutional arena. An even more basic example can be seen in constitutional designs proposed by those who place the highest value on liberty and want a minimalist government. They would require large majorities to pass laws, would place constitutional limits on deficits and debt, and usually favour a decentralized form of government, believing it would mean less government. Therefore constitutional design is also about policy choices. The question is do we want to put social policy choices explicitly in a constitution?

The strongest argument in favour of a social charter is that economic and political forces are changing and this requires a constitutional change in the foundations of social policy. People and economic capital are becoming more mobile; if their alternative destinations have fewer social programs (and lower taxes) this may pressure governments to cut back on social programs, or set provinces against one another competing for productive resources through lower taxes. As a counterbalance to these pressures, all regions might agree to entrench social programs.

There can be little dispute about the changing economic and political forces — but is a social charter the best way for Canada to respond? There are the already mentioned problems of letting courts (or other non-parliamentary bodies) determine social policy and of diminishing Parliament's power of the purse. There is also the danger that a social charter will lock us into current ways of doing things, just when preservation of our social programs requires radical rethinking. Consider a number of examples.

The existing *Canada Health Act* contains a number of norms or standards to which provinces must conform in order to receive federal transfers. These are: comprehensiveness — the plan has to cover all medically required services; universality — the services must be provided to all residents; portability — benefits must be portable between provinces; public administration — the plan has to be administered on a strictly nonprofit basis; and accessibility — access to services should not be inhibited by such practices as the charging of fees. The Ontario discussion of a social charter suggests these health principles might be generalized to cover other social programs. Every provincial government is struggling with rising health care costs, struggling to find ways to contain costs yet preserve service levels. No one has yet found an acceptable trade-off, and innovation and creativity are desperately needed. The situation in Canada is especially acute because of our debt crisis. Perhaps part of a solution would be to stop financing certain medical services, or to allow private-sector administration of parts of the plan, or to charge some people user fees. But these options are forbidden under the *Canada Health Act* and might be forbidden under a social charter.

The threat to our social programs is not that a neoconservative coalition has captured the political system as some have argued. The threat is the requirement for fiscal prudence and our lower rate of economic growth and competing demands for public funds. If we accept the reality of these constraints, as many voters now do, the need is for innovation. Just as provincial innovation created national consensus to build our welfare state, so we might turn again to provincial innovation to find the means to sustain it in the years ahead. A social charter might reduce flexibility when it is most needed.

Some of our most basic values may have to change as we accept our limited resources and search to find a new social contract in an increasingly competitive world. Universality has been a hallmark of our social programs, because benefits were a right of citizenship and did not flow from charity. But universality is expensive. Could we not devise a new right of citizenship, giving benefits only to the needy and not to all? Much of our social safety net, from unemployment insurance to provincial equalization, provides security of place. But this retards labour mobility and creates transfer dependency of entire regions. Could we not revise our social safety net to provide greater security of person and less security of place? The challenge to our social programs is real and belongs in our constitutional debate, but whether the best response is a social charter remains to be decided.

Alone among the constitutional models, the Beaudoin-Dobbie Report recommends a social charter, labelling it a social covenant. The covenant would commit all governments "to social programs which Canadians see as part of their national identity." The commitments express goals, not rights. Elected governments, rather than courts, would have authority to decide how they can best be fulfilled. The social covenant and a commitment to the economic union would be joined in Section 36 as central tenets of governance, common to all Canadians. The proposed covenant contains the norms of the *Canada Health Act* and so reduces flexibility in reforming health financing. Quebec will likely have great reservations about a social covenant common to all Canadians.

6

Two Countries:
ROC and Quebec

There are times, and they occur with discouraging frequency, when the aspirations of Quebec and of the rest of Canada seem irreconcilable. There are many people within Quebec who reached that conclusion years ago and want Quebec to be an independent nation. For the first time in our history, a substantial number of people outside Quebec are publicly agreeing. Without rancour and without casting blame, they are saying "bon voyage." There is an eerie fatigue in the general public as we approach the 1992 Quebec referendum. The "constitutional reform" we ultimately consider may be the creation of two new nations.

Could ROC Survive?
Whether federalist or sovereignist, the people of Quebec have always had a strong sense of themselves. The government of Quebec could smoothly become a national government. The transition would not be so easy for what remains of Canada. We do not even have a name for Canada without Quebec. Is it Canada Outside Quebec (COQ), or English Canada, or Canada Without Quebec (CWQ) or the Rest of Canada (ROC)? For no particular reason, save euphony, let's use the term ROC.

In both the Quebec sovereignist movement and the "bon voyage" movement, there is an assumption that after Quebec's unilateral declaration of independence there would exist an entity for Quebec to negotiate with. This is not obvious. It is ironic that Quebec sovereignists assume ROC would emerge as a cohesive nation, but it is consistent with the Quebec view of Canada as a pact between English and French.

But how would ROC's national institutions function if Quebec declared independence? ROC does not exist as a nation. ROC does not have any national institutions. Under the constitution, seventy-five members of the House of Commons are elected from Quebec, including the current prime minister and some members of the cabinet. If these members were removed from the House, the Progressive Conservative Party would no longer command a majority and would have to elect a new leader. The Senate and the Supreme Court similarly have members from Quebec and would have to be reconfigured. Until such time as our constitution is amended, however, the Parliament of Canada includes members and senators from Quebec. Therefore, during negotiations with Quebec, ROC either would be represented by the existing Government of Canada, a government without political legitimacy, or by a government excluding Quebec members without constitutional legitimacy. If Quebec becomes independent, two new nations will be created. ROC will have to create its own constitution, its own federal system and its own division of powers.

ROC has scarcely thought about how it should organize itself. Quebec has been following an explicit two-track strategy, one examining renewed federalism and the other examining independence. ROC is, with few exceptions, only debating renewed federalism. This is understandable. Many in ROC believe "my Canada includes Quebec." From Champlain to the coureurs de bois to the empire of the St. Lawrence to Maurice Richard to Michel Tremblay is an unbroken line of history. The struggle to reconcile English and French is a defining national characteristic. For them, Canada without Quebec is inconceivable and to openly speculate about it will be taken as a rejection of Quebec.

But by October 1992, ROC may have to create itself. It is dangerously naive to assume that a coherent, stable nation would emerge quickly. Consider three speculations about the nature of ROC that have been published.

One, under the title *Deconfederation: Canada Without Quebec,* is more than just optimistic. It argues ROC would be better off. "The departure of Quebec would provide a magnificent opportunity for Canadians to undertake a general restructuring of the political order in which they live ... The departure of Quebec may galvanize Canadians to tackle their own real and pressing problems." The authors, David J. Bercuson and Barry Cooper, two university professors from the West, recognize that it is not up to them "to write their [new] nation's constitution. But we are willing to give it a try." Their new constitution would create an indissoluble political union, a free-market economic union, without bilingualism or state support for religious schools, with strong provinces and a Triple-E Senate, and resting on the bedrock of a Charter of Rights and Freedoms guaranteeing individual liberty as its highest good.

Is this the constitution that could generate a consensus in ROC? Our constitution in 1867 guaranteed Catholic schools the rights they had at Confederation. Would Catholic parents agree to give up the rights they now enjoy in order to achieve equality for all before the law? This proposed constitution values individual liberty above all while our current constitution speaks of peace, order and good government. Canadian history and politics are filled with examples of support for mutual sharing and for collective rights. There are many in ROC who support collective rights and might even prefer scrapping the Charter and returning to the supremacy of Parliament.

An Ontario-based economist, Dan Usher, recently proposed in *Economic Dimensions of Constitutional Change* that ROC should be a unitary state without provinces. He noted that Sir John A. Macdonald's vision of Canada was of "one government and one parliament, legislating for the whole of these peoples. It would be the best, the cheapest, the most vigorous and the strongest system of government we could adopt. But ... we found that such a system was impracticable. In the first place, it would not meet the assent of the people of Lower Canada." If Quebec were gone, Usher asserted, the argument for a unitary state would re-emerge. He goes on to support the argument on many grounds, including the absence of provincial cultures. It is not that ROC is especially homogeneous but that the cultural differences are not primarily along provincial lines. "If Quebec seceded and if English Canada did somehow manage to reconstruct itself as a unitary state, the people of English Canada would have little or no nostalgia for their provincial governments. Within three weeks, provincial governments and provincial entities would be forgotten altogether."

Perhaps such writing could only come from Ontario, but it illustrates the significant differences within ROC. On the issue of centralization verses decentralization, we overemphasize the tension between Ottawa and Quebec City. This tension will remain in ROC, as will the tension about individual versus collective rights, and struggles over equalization, social programs, the debt, and aboriginal self-government. A constitution for ROC will not be easy to write, especially because of the jolt of Quebec's separation. This would not be evolution from the status quo. The creation of ROC is the creation of a new country. All existing commitments would be up for reconsideration.

A third speculation about the shape of ROC was undertaken in Alberta. Economists gathered to consider the economic implications of alternative constitutional arrangements. The options analysed were: the status quo, a more centralized Canada (with Quebec), a more decentralized Canada (with Quebec), an independent western Canada and an independent Alberta. ROC was not explicitly analysed as an option. With everything up for grabs, the West is considering its prospects as an independent country. In some studies, an independent West ranked ahead of the status quo and a more centralized Canada. Even the Economic Council of Canada analysed a confederation of regions as a constitutional option. In more provocative language, this option is a confederation of independent nations.

Shuddering centrifugal political forces would be set loose as each province undertook a fundamental reconsideration of its economic interests. The Ontario economy is linked predominantly to the eastern U.S. economy and to Quebec. British Columbia's economy is linked to the western U.S. and the Pacific Rim. Alberta and British Columbia have long been major contributors to equalization but feel they have not been full beneficiaries of the larger whole. The centre and the West might go their own ways.

Quebec has minutely examined the economic consequences of separation, and federalists have tried to highlight how high are the costs and how great the risks. But costs and risks for Quebec are often mirrored by the costs and risks for ROC.

The greatest cost and gravest risk would come from balkanization of the Canadian economic union. There could be trade disruptions between ROC and Quebec; the more acrimonious the separation, the greater the disruptions. However there would be powerful balkanizing forces within ROC if a highly decentralized nation emerged. (They would be even greater in a multi-nation outcome.) Many provinces have nondiversified economies and would face considerable political pressure to support their export-oriented industries. One can think of the forestry industry in B.C., oil in Alberta and autos in Ontario. As subsidies and special protection emerged, a tit-for-tat squabble might follow. The reduction in interprovincial trade and heightened regional conflict would undermine the basis for interprovincial redistribution. One does not have to be an alarmist to foresee restrictions on labour and capital mobility emerging as well. The economic costs to citizens of ROC could be very high. They are impossible to quantify but might run as high as 3–4 percent of GDP — akin to another recession like the one we are experiencing in the early 1990s.

ROC would also lose international influence and prestige, not just because the absolute size of its economy would be smaller (about the size of Spain's) but also because it would be one fragment of a failed experiment — Canada. All our international treaties would have to be renegotiated, including the FTA and even perhaps the Auto Pact. Our power in these renegotiations would be much diminished.

Canadian historians have always written, with evident pride, that Canada is an economically illogical and disparate nation whose creation and longevity are major accomplishments. If we chip off one quarter of the whole, the rest might break asunder. Even if it does not, there will be turmoil before stability, and ROC's standard of living will fall.

The Terms of Separation

Some people speak of a friendly, smooth breakup. This is nonsense. A breakup will be acrimonious and messy. Two new nations (perhaps more) will be created and these nations will have different interests. The leadership of both nations will pursue their nation's self interests aggressively and vigorously. Both nations would, of course, seek to maintain harmonious economic relations, but that does not mean the status quo will prevail. There would be new arrangements to put in place and new national interests at play.

Normally, negotiations between nations are tough but civil. However passions can flare and overwhelm what would be in the economic interests of both parties. The current situation in Europe offers Canada examples of harmonious integration of nations and fractious disintegration of nations. It is impossible to predict whether passion would overwhelm rationality in the relations between Quebec and ROC. The majority of people in both nations and their national leaderships will find it in their interest to establish friendly economic relations, and to create economic stability as quickly as possible. For obvious reasons this view has been strenuously advanced by the Parti Québécois.

But each and every citizen will not favour harmony. Examples can be easily proposed. Imagine an English-speaking businesswoman in Montreal who has established her own successful company. She is a Canadian citizen on the day before the Quebec referendum and votes no. But the majority of Quebecers choose independence. She wishes to remain a Canadian and asks her national government (ROC) for economic assistance to move her business to Toronto. It is one of the highest duties of a nation to assist its citizens in foreign lands. How could ROC refuse her request? But a trade treaty between the nations would surely forbid subsidies which help businesses to leave the other nation.

Take another example. Suppose the Cree in northern Quebec ask to remain in ROC. Their right of self-determination is as valid as the right of French-speaking Quebecers. Their land is as much a historic homeland. Furthermore, many people would argue the land belongs in ROC because it became part of the province of Quebec after Confederation and only because Quebec was a province in Canada.

Or imagine if part of a regiment of the Canadian armed forces stationed in Quebec decides it wishes to remain with ROC, along with the tanks it operates. The separation negotiations had allocated the men, women and equipment to Quebec. What could ROC do in response to calls from its soldiers on foreign soil? National passion is highly contagious and a few hotheads might become many. Rational economic interests might not prevail in these cases.

The weight of Canadian history presses heavily toward the conclusion that moderation would prevail. The moderating forces might even become overwhelmingly stronger than they appear today, because Canadians are intensely proud of our traditions of tolerance and accommodation. The acrimonious breakup of the nation would stain this heritage. If Quebec chose sovereignty, there might be a move to create a new framework, consistent with tolerance *and* Quebec independence. Canada could again offer the world a model of accommodation to diversity in a larger whole.

Although the desire to preserve friendly economic relations would exist on both sides, there is no escaping that two nations would confront one another with differing economic interests. The most contentious areas will be division of the debt, trade relations and use of the currency.

The national debt of the Government of Canada is now over $400 billion. This would have to be divided between ROC and Quebec, as would the national assets. There is no established international law on debt and asset division. There are many issues to negotiate, on which people in good conscience would disagree. Quebec would have some leverage because the public debt is an obligation of Canada and technically would be ROC's responsibility. However, Quebec would continue to require foreign capital and could not risk being seen as shirking its obligations. Also, Quebec would need to maintain close economic ties with ROC. There would be similar pressures on ROC to calm foreign bond holders and to maintain friendly economic ties with Quebec. Both parties would want a quick, clean resolution and would seek to convince themselves and the world that their position was fair.

It should be remembered this is not entirely an additional debt burden to the Quebec economy. Citizens of Quebec would no longer pay taxes to Ottawa. What they once paid to

Ottawa to service the national debt would be paid to Quebec City to service the transferred share of national debt.

The Bélanger-Campeau Commission sets out a framework for calculating the division of assets and debt and Quebec's opening negotiating position. The Commission divides federal liabilities into three components: liabilities incurred to acquire assets; liabilities related to future pension obligations; and liabilities incurred in the past provision of goods and services. There is a different system proposed for dividing each component.

The debt related to assets is to be divided according to who gets the asset. The Commission identifies three types of federal asset: financial assets (including gold held by the Bank of Canada); real assets (mainly land, buildings and equipment owned by the federal government); and federal government enterprises.

Quebec proposes to take no financial assets (and so no corresponding share of the debt), to take all real assets within its borders, and to choose selectively from federal government enterprises. These claims give Quebec lower than its per capita share of the assets and so lower than its per capita share of the debt. Each choice is contentious and there will be special problems around how to value real assets and government enterprises.

The pension liabilities are for federal public servants, armed forces personnel, RCMP, MPs and federal judges. These liabilities are divided in some cases by current place of residence, and in some cases by Quebec's share of Canada's population (25.4 percent).

The remaining liability, by far the largest and most important, relates to past federal expenditures. Bélanger-Campeau takes a forward-looking approach and argues current debt would have had to be paid out of future taxes. Quebec is forecast to contribute 22.8 percent of future federal taxes and therefore would accept about 22.8 percent of the remaining liability.

But there are other quite different approaches. Another approach is backward looking and argues that the debt was accumulated because of past federal activities and if a province is to leave, it must pay off its accumulated net benefits. Calculation of these would be complex and controversial, but would assign Quebec a much higher share of the debt. A third alternative is neither forward looking nor backward looking. The nation's assets and debts are seen as a collective responsibility of all citizens and would be divided on a per capita basis. Quebec would take about 25.4 percent of the debt, its share of total population.

The Bélanger-Campeau position is the most advantageous for Quebec, and the historical benefits approach the least advantageous. Quebec's share of debt would be $66 billion according to Bélanger-Campeau; on the basis of population its share would be $100 billion; and according to the historical benefits approach it would be $128 billion. These are huge differences.

Even with agreement about the share, there are complex transition problems about how Quebec could take over responsibility for billions of dollars of debt. The current bond owners hold Government of Canada securities and would not accept a simple swap for Quebec bonds. Quebec most certainly could not go to the market and borrow, let us say, $100 billion.

Perhaps Quebec could just send ROC the interest due on Quebec's share of the debt; Jacques Parizeau has proposed this. But ROC, so recently jilted by Quebec, would never agree. Quebec would retain, in effect, ROC's higher credit rating. Furthermore ROC would still be liable in the unlikely event that Quebec were to default on its interest payments.

Even if Quebec paid interest until the Canadian debt came due, there would be problems. The national debt is not long-term debt, half of it is short-term and most of the rest has a maturity of under seven years. An independent Quebec would have to develop a market for $100 billion in debt within seven years — a formidable task.

Trade arrangements between ROC and Quebec and the rest of the world would have to be established quickly in order to maintain as much economic stability as possible. Common sense says we should maintain the status quo in trading relations, but common sense could easily be drowned out. The voices demanding mercantilist trade policies will be strong. For example, Quebec may want to flex its new sovereignty. However, it may prove that independence combined with trade integration gives Quebec no more sovereignty than it now enjoys, and ironically Quebec's economic sovereignty may even be diminished. But this will only be learned after lengthy trade skirmishes. Or another example, even when a trade policy generates a net gain for society, some individuals are winners and some are losers — and the potential losers demand help. The political economy of trade policy is a struggle among potential winners and losers. The free trade we now have within Canada would not come easily between nations. People more often vote for trade protection and retaliation to protect their existing jobs than for freer trade to get lower prices and economic growth in the future.

The most important issue will be Quebec-ROC trade agreements. These will be the cornerstone of relations between the two and the rest of the world.

About 35 percent of the total gross output (which includes both intermediate and final goods) of the Quebec economy is sold outside its borders. Of these exports, 58 percent are sold in ROC, 31 percent are sold in the United States and 11 percent in the rest of the world. More than half of the trade with ROC is with Ontario. The percentages are about the same for the origins of goods and services consumed in Quebec. An independent Quebec would be a trading nation, like the small countries of Europe. Its most important trading partner by an overwhelming margin would be ROC, and then the United States. The dream of Quebec developing trading alternatives in Europe is naive and distant.

The trading situation of ROC is not symmetric. About 26 percent of ROC's total gross output would be sold outside its borders. Of these exports, 61 percent would be sold in the United States, 18 percent in Quebec and 21 percent in other nations. ROC's most important trading partner would be overwhelmingly the United States, with Quebec a distant second, and the rest of the world combined more important than Quebec. As a trading partner Quebec would need ROC more than ROC would need Quebec.

In trading matters, Quebec would be to ROC as Canada is to the United States. It is a tragic reflection of our two solitudes that English Canada's jitters about entering a free trade agreement with the United States were not more sympathetically understood in Quebec.

After Quebec and ROC have sat at the negotiating table,

what sort of trade deal is likely to emerge? Quebec could quickly enter the General Agreement on Tariffs and Trade (GATT) as a successor state, and so the GATT rules would be both a starting position and a fallback if negotiations failed. If a free-trade area were negotiated, there would be no tariffs between the nations but each nation would retain sovereignty to set external tariffs. National frontiers would be established and customs offices put in place to verify that rules of origin on the goods had been complied with. If a customs union were negotiated, ROC and Quebec would establish a common external tariff and trade policy, and there would be no need for border points. An economic and monetary union would approximate what we have today, but it is unlikely it could be negotiated in the short run.

Achieving only a free-trade area is almost unthinkable. The trade disruption of customs checks along the ROC-Quebec borders would be too large. A customs union is the most likely outcome, but even that would be tough. Both Quebec and ROC face problems that the sovereignist and "bon voyage" movements have chosen to ignore. These problems deserve more attention.

Quebec would enter negotiations as a nation, not as a province. In trading treaties, national governments have generally not imposed obligations on their subnational governments. Many of Quebec's current economic policies under Quebec, Inc. are possible as a province but not acceptable for a nation. For example, the current procurement policies of Quebec City and Hydro-Québec are allowable under the GATT code as long as Quebec is a province, but would

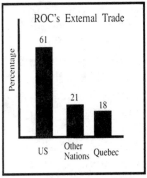

Source: A Joint Venture, 1991
ECC Annual Review

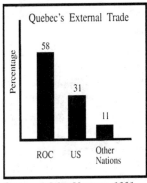

Source: A Joint Venture, 1991
ECC Annual Review

not be if Quebec became a nation. In negotiations with ROC, Quebec could only address programs of the national government, not of the provinces. For example, Quebec's agricultural policies would be on the table but Alberta's or Ontario's would not.

ROC for its part would have huge problems establishing its negotiating position. The political-constitutional crisis has been mentioned, but let's assume it was overcome and a trade team was appointed. The Ontario economy is closely integrated with Quebec's, but the West has few ties with Quebec and trade disruptions would affect them only indirectly. The West might push for "hard-ball" negotiations while Ontario opted for "pragmatism." The Maritimes would watch nervously as the vigorous pursuit of regional interests endangered the national commitment to equalization and integration. Canada has always had a centre-periphery tension. The centre-periphery tensions would not go away in ROC, indeed they would get worse because the dislocation of separation would mean all past deals were off.

The ROC and Quebec negotiators would each come to the bargaining table with a list of irritants to remove. The customs union requires a common external tariff and external quotas. ROC would try to lower the tariff on items produced mainly in Quebec, such as textiles and clothing. Quebec would try to maintain the external quotas on dairy products since Quebec produces almost 50 percent of Canada's market at prices almost twice the import price. Obviously ROC would favour a lower quota. And so it would go through each commodity.

There would also have to be rules on government purchasing, trade in services, investment screening and financial services. Most controversial of all would be a subsidies code. Under international trade law, countries are free to levy countervailing duties against subsidized imports that injure domestic producers. A tit-for-tat trade war could easily result.

There would have to be a standing tribunal to monitor the agreement and to negotiate further integration. This is a pure extra cost to dividing into two countries, because previously the trade was not under agreement. These costs would partially offset any gains from removing the overlap of federal and provincial jurisdictions.

After ROC and Quebec had settled their arrangements, they could turn to negotiations with their other major trading partner, the United States. It is unlikely the U.S. would want to enter separate negotiations with Quebec and ROC until their mutual arrangements were clarified or to enter trilateral discussions dominated by Quebec-ROC issues.

The existing Free Trade Agreement (FTA) with the United States is not a framework that could automatically be transformed into a three-party agreement. Quebec would not automatically be a party to the FTA and would have to apply for inclusion. Basically, Quebec would step from subnational status to the status of nation and therefore would have to accept national obligations. Many Quebec, Inc. practices would come under review. Any trade agreement is a complex trade-off of political forces and leverage. Within each country there are conflicting interests to resolve, depending on the political power of the interests. Between countries there are also conflicting interests to resolve, depending on the power of the nations. The political powers would shift as Canada split into ROC and Quebec, and the international power would shift as a bilateral agreement became trilateral. The only party with increased power would be the United States. ROC would try to retain the FTA without renegotiation, but the U.S. might prefer a completely new deal. It is hard to imagine that the U.S. would let Quebec or ROC improve its position under a renegotiation.

The currency for Quebec is the third economic arrangement to reach, but the initiative would be mainly Quebec's. ROC would continue to use the Canadian dollar supervised by the Bank of Canada. Quebec would have five options: use the Canadian dollar with monetary policy and financial market regulation shared between ROC and Quebec; unilaterally use the Canadian dollar, but let ROC administer the monetary union; create a Quebec currency pegged to the Canadian dollar or to the U.S. dollar; unilaterally use the U.S. dollar; or create a Quebec currency with a flexible exchange rate.

A nation's currency and its flag are the most highly visible symbols of sovereignty. However, a currency is one symbol of nationhood Quebec is willing to forego. A common currency hugely facilitates the economic integration on which ROC and Quebec depend because the currency reduces the transactions costs and removes the exchange rate risk in economic exchange. Furthermore, our existing financial system is Canada-wide with the same banks operating in all provinces. There is a national clearing system. Whatever symbolic and economic gains are to be had from a separate currency for Quebec, they are marginal compared to the risks in fragmenting the monetary union. Economists, bankers, and business people, both inside and outside Quebec, are in agreement: it would be in everyone's interest for Quebec to use the Canadian dollar and for Quebec and ROC to form a monetary union. The contentious issue would be how (or if) Quebec would participate in monetary policy decisions and the regulation of financial markets.

There have been doomsday scenarios of ROC refusing use of the Canadian dollar, of a separate currency and of competitive devaluations, but the consensus is that they are improbable. ROC could not credibly refuse use of the Canadian dollar knowing that Quebec has a fallback of a currency pegged to the U.S. dollar. And ROC has nothing to gain from fragmenting the monetary union. However, designing the joint monetary policy for the two nations will be excruciatingly difficult and contentious. In a transition to sovereignty, the shared dollar would likely fall and interest rates rise, possibly precipitating severe stagflation.

Quebec would no doubt prefer a binational panel to run monetary policy and financial markets but ROC would resist. What would likely emerge is a complex new supranational structure in which the interests of Quebec and ROC, and all the provinces of ROC would be represented. The Governor of the Bank of Canada would retain independence. Whether Quebec would gain sovereignty compared to the current proposals to increase regional representation in the Bank of Canada and against the background of globalizing financial markets is difficult to say. Any gain would be marginal, but no doubt the Quebec government would need a new bureau of monetary affairs.

Is an Independent Quebec Economically Viable?

If the dominant question about ROC is its constitutional structure, there is an equally dominant question asked of an independent Quebec: Is it economically viable? The simple answer is — yes, of course. Quebec would have an economy about the size of Denmark or Austria's. It would be the thirteenth largest economy among the twenty-four in the OECD. There is no international evidence that small countries are worse off. Quebec has natural resources, a relatively diversified economy, a skilled labour force and an experienced managerial class. It has stable government and a high level of public services and public infrastructure. Quebec would not be impoverished. ROC would have a 12 percent higher per capita income than Quebec, but using purchasing power parity conversions, Quebec would be the third richest OECD country behind the U.S. and ROC.

Viability is really not the important question, however, because a viable economy could still mean a declining economy. The important questions are: What will be the short-run transition costs of Quebec becoming a sovereign state and what will be the long-run effect on Quebec citizens' standard of living?

The important determinants of Quebec's short-run economic prospects are the separation agreements on territory, division of the national debt, trade arrangements and currency, and how international financial markets react to the separation. If the inevitable acrimony overwhelms the economic self-interests of both nations, and negotiations break down, Quebec would suffer. But ROC would also suffer, especially Ontario, which sends 20 percent of its exports to Quebec. The degree of acrimony and its influence on negotiations are impossible to predict. The best working assumption is probably of tough, civil but slow negotiation, with increased uncertainty about Quebec's economic prospects.

There would be significant transition costs. There would have to be painful adjustments in the government budget as a sovereign Quebec assumed all federal activities. The Quebec government would take over all federal program expenditures in Quebec, all federal taxation in Quebec and, depending upon its share of the national debt, Quebec would face extra public debt charges. It is enormously complex and controversial to calculate Quebec's share of these three components. For the sake of illustration, let us assume Quebec's share of each is equal to its share of Canadian GDP—23.4 percent. A sovereign Quebec would take on an extra budgetary deficit of $7.14 billion. This is the simple arithmetic of the Canadian federal fiscal crisis. It cannot be escaped through sovereignty, and Quebec recognizes that if it takes over the federal domain, it takes over a deficit as well. But this extra deficit would leave the Quebec economy no more indebted than it is today, because the deficit is only the result of consolidating federal activities in Quebec into the Quebec budget.

The movement to sovereignty, however, is more than a straightforward consolidation; other adjustments are needed. There are two obvious budgetary implications of independence. Quebec receives slightly more than a 23.4 percent share of federal expenditures, while slightly less than a 23.4 percent share of federal revenues is collected in Quebec. For example, under the Equalization Program Quebec receives over 47 percent of the payments. Quebec contributes only 22.8 percent of federal taxes. A takeover of federal activities would imply a greater deficit than $7.14 billion. This extra deficit is equivalent to the net transfer Quebec currently receives because of federalism. It is large, likely in the order of $1–3 billion dollars, but not nearly as large as many people in ROC perceive it to be, and it has been declining in recent years. A further adjustment should be made because Quebec will pay a higher risk premium on its debt than the federal government does. There is already a difference between the interest rates on Canada bonds and Quebec bonds. The spread will increase further

Additions to Quebec Deficit
($ Millions)

	Total Federal Budget 90/91				Quebec Share
Program Spending	108,300	x	.234	=	25,342
Public Debt Charges	42,950	x	.234	=	10,050
Budgetary Revenues	120,750	x	.234	=	28,256
Federal Deficit	-30,500				-7,136
			Extra Risk Premium		- 1,000
			Lost Federalism		- 2,000
			Extra Quebec Deficit		-10,136

because Quebec will be a high debt country, whose economic prospects are uncertain, and with a less diversified economy than Canada's. The extra risk premium would add another $700 million to $1 billion to the deficit.

The direction, if not absolute size, of these modifications are obvious and generally accepted. Further modifications are more contentious. Calculations by the Secretariat of the Bélanger-Campeau Commission emphasized the savings from removing duplication and overlap. But there are also new expenses of coordination between national governments and some activities may be more expensive because of lost economies of scale. These were ignored. Furthermore, no adjustment was made for reduced tax collections because of trade disruptions, emigration and reduced investment.

The Bélanger-Campeau Commission estimated an independent Quebec's budget deficit would increase only $160 million over a consolidated position. This low estimate arises because it assumed a very favourable division of assets and debt, no extra risk premium, savings from reduced overlap and no dislocation costs. Another estimate of "parting as friends" calculated an extra deficit of $4.5 billion over a consolidated budget. This calculation divided assets and debt using the share of GDP (23.4 percent) and added amounts due to a risk premium on Quebec debt and dislocation shocks. The latter estimate strove to be reasonable and sympathetic to Quebec. It is more realistic than Bélanger-Campeau. But let us split the difference and assume the sovereignty deficit is $2.2 billion as several Quebec economists have suggested.

A sovereign Quebec would have a high deficit and a high debt. The paramount task of its government would be to reduce its deficits and set out a credible medium-term fiscal plan. There would have to be an immediate deficit reduction of $1–2 billion. The package of tax increases and expenditure cuts will be especially difficult because of a possible emigration of firms and people. Other jurisdictions will try to attract these people and firms, and most have lower tax rates, especially in the United States. Also, there will be acute political pressures on Quebec to visibly use its new economic sovereignty. Any group in Quebec that is hurt by the transition to independence will surely demand government assistance.

Even under the assumption that a sovereign Quebec could

manage its finances and quickly establish international credibility, there would be short-run economic losses for Quebec. These short-run losses have been variously estimated at $1,000–$2,000 per Quebecer or 4–8 percent of real GDP. For perspective on these numbers, the 1981–1982 recession reduced Canadian real GDP by 5.2 percent from peak to trough and the current recession reduced GDP by 2.8 percent. The sovereignty shock on the Quebec economy would be severe, especially coming after a deep recession.

The toughest question is whether Quebec's economy will resume its expected long-run growth after the shock, or whether the shock will reduce its long-run growth prospects. One school of thought emphasizes declining prospects, seeing an emigration of head offices and people (especially talented, ambitious people seeking a better future), reduced investment and difficulty attracting new immigrants. These set up a vicious circle of higher taxes, lower public services, and more emigration. Another school of thought is optimistic. It notes that Quebec has suffered two great shocks over the last twenty years — the collapse of its old manufacturing sector and the departure of firms and people following the election of the Parti Québécois. Despite these shocks, Quebec's economy has grown as fast as Canada's over the last decade. Quebec's manufacturing productivity grew more rapidly than Ontario's and the unemployment gap narrowed. Indeed, Quebec's economic dynamism was a remarkable feature of the 1980s. This school sees long-run prospects as unchanged, even enhanced with a decline in linguistic tensions, greater policy coherence and the ability of Quebec, as a cohesive society, to make difficult economic adjustments that Canada could not make.

Perhaps the economic shock to Quebec will pale beside the disruption in ROC as it struggles to create itself. A constitutional crisis might erupt pitting the West against Ontario, challenging the national commitment to redistribution, all amidst bitter recriminations about who caused the breakup of Canada. Quebec might emerge as a pluralist society, so self-confident of its linguistic future that language laws are relaxed and the anglophone minority is celebrated. In this scenario, Toronto's best and brightest move to Montreal.

The dreams of a renascent Quebec are about as likely as the nightmares of a Quebec slide into poverty. The real future will be less dramatic: a hard slog for Quebec, and for ROC, just to equal their current economic prospects. Both countries will need foreign financing, and both countries will face a certain amount of turmoil and uncertainty. Foreign investors (like any citizens putting their savings in a trust company or a bank) do not like turmoil and uncertainty around their investments.

The European Experience

In the debates over Canada's constitutional and economic future, reference is often made to the European Community (EC). The European experience has been especially cited in Quebec. Many believe that the Community is purely an economic enterprise, and that it demonstrates nations of diverse cultures can join together in an economic union while retaining their political sovereignty. These beliefs are implicit in many discussions of renewed federalism, as various decentralist and asymmetric proposals are considered, and they are explicit in discussion about potential arrangements between ROC and an independent Quebec. The Parti Québécois favours Quebec as a sovereign nation state, joined in an economic and monetary union with Canada in a North American free trade area.

The European Economic Community began in 1957 with six member states and now includes twelve members under the more general title of the European Community. The EC will likely engage in some "widening" through the addition of new members, but its more important project is "deepening" the integration. In 1987 a new treaty, the *Single European Act*, came into force, committing the EC to a market "without internal frontiers" by 31 December 1992. A background document for the 1992 program identified almost 300 steps necessary to remove all barriers to the free movement of goods, people, services and capital. Most of the steps have now been taken.

The first misconception in Canada is that the EC is purely an economic enterprise. Of course, it is partly an economic enterprise. Europeans recognize that there are gains in income from the increased competition and scale economies that economic integration creates. This recognition was pressed home in the 1970s when the Europeans felt they might be left behind by the larger and more dynamic U.S. and Japanese economies. But the fundamental drive to economic integration was not economic. The origins of the Community lie in the European wars of 1914 and 1939. There was a profound desire to stop wars on the European continent, and economic integration and cooperation were the means. Also, Europeans — Dutch, Germans, French, Italians — believe themselves part of a community living in a "common European home." They have a dream of a European family, and the dream is more real than ever before.

This makes the European experience inapplicable to Canada in a painfully poignant way. We seem to want to separate into enclaves. We hear few evocations of a "common Canadian home."

The second misconception is that European economic integration is being accomplished with no loss of national sovereignty. Nothing could be further from the truth. Economic integration can only be achieved with some political integration.

The 1992 project is accompanied by a move toward a monetary union and a European political union. Political union is, of course, a long way off and being approached with a mix of optimism and trepidation. But long before political union, the EC has established central authority for joint decision making. It created a number of supranational institutions of considerable power. EC legislation is enacted by a Council of Ministers made up of twelve ministers from the member states. For general matters this would be the foreign ministers, but on specific issues they might be the finance ministers or transportation ministers or environment ministers. Even more powerful is the European Commission, a sort of executive with broad powers of initiative. The Commissioners are appointed for a four-year term and the treaty stipulates they shall "be completely independent in the performance of their duties; they shall neither seek nor take instruction from any government or any other body." It was the Commission that prepared the list of 300 steps necessary for the 1992 project, and it is the Commission that is working on monetary and political union. The Commission has real power. For example, all forms of assistance to industry by the member nations are prohibited unless approved by the Commission. The Commission must rely on member states to implement many of its directives, but the European Court of Justice was created to ensure the treaties are observed by member states. The Court has established the principle that the directives of Community institutions have power over the conflicting laws of member states. And national courts have been willing to hold member states to their treaty obligations and to enforce Community directives. It is generally agreed that the European Court was essential for economic integration.

These supranational institutions have worked both for negative integration — the removal of tariffs, quotas and other trade barriers such as industrial subsidies — and for positive integration — the creation of common business framework laws, labour laws, and community-wide standards for health care, schooling, pensions and benefits such as maternity leave. It is recognized that the coming monetary union will require coordinated fiscal policies, with limits on national deficits and debt.

Both Quebec and ROC would like to preserve our existing economic and monetary union. The lessons of the EC are clear. This can only be done by creating supranational institutions, by transferring considerable sovereignty to these institutions and by mutually agreeing to extensive positive integration.

The liaison between ROC and Quebec would be highly unstable. This is not just because of the history leading up to the break; bilateral arrangements between unequal-sized partners are by nature unstable. The nature of representation in the supranational institutions would surely be controversial. Quebec would prefer an equal number of representatives from Quebec and from ROC. After all, there are two sovereign nations coming together. But this would be unacceptable to ROC. The national institutions of Canada where Quebec has about one quarter of the central representatives would be replaced by supranational institutions where Quebec would have one half of the representatives. If the representation were based on population or economic size, it would be unacceptable to Quebec because it would be too much like our present system. The instability is especially acute for a monetary union — the larger party has little incentive to give up any control and the smaller party would not want to be a constant supplicant.

The European Community's supranational institutions are dominated by the unelected Commission and Court of Justice. More and more power is held by bureaucrats, not elected representatives. The European Parliament is mainly consultative, it is not a legislature and has no independent taxing powers. Europeans refer to this as "the democratic deficit." The citizens of ROC and of Quebec would probably find this level of bureaucratic control unacceptable, especially because one or the other would perceive themselves as unfairly represented in the bureaucracy.

The European Community and its supranational institutions are in transition; this is not the final extent of integration. ROC and Quebec should not believe that the current European model could be a permanent arrangement for us. As positive integration proceeds in Europe, as common fiscal, defence, foreign and social policies are developed, the democratic deficit will have to be erased. This is the task of the European Political Union. The term "federalism" is still eschewed, but a federalism is coming.

The debate is shifting toward questions such as what powers should be assigned to the supranational Parliament and what powers left with the nations states? How should the economic union be policed — by the supranational Parliament, by an administrative tribunal or by coordination among ministers of the nation states? Does this sound familiar? It should. Europe is moving to what Canada now has. Substitute the words national Parliament for supranational Parliament, the word province for nation state, and their debate is our debate over renewed federalism. In the long run, the sovereignty of the constituent parts may be quite similar. However there is one vital difference, symbolic, but vital nonetheless. In Canada the local parts are provinces; in Europe they are nations. This symbolic difference is the heart of the Quebec sovereignist dream.

7

Afterword

Where do we go from here? It is easy to be pessimistic. The federal government's strategy for moving the constitutional debate to a conclusion changes day by day. No one seems to be in charge or to know where we are headed. Some of the tough issues of this constitutional round are still unresolved. None of the alternative federalisms commands clear consensus.

However, let us be optimistic — but also candid and realistic. We face an enormously difficult task. Keith Banting and Richard Simeon state: "The demand for constitutional change itself represents lack of consensus about some important aspects of the system; but since rules governing constitutional change normally require a high degree of consensus it is often impossible to mobilize sufficient comment to bring the issues to a close. Lack of consensus makes constitutional change necessary. The same lack makes resolution supremely difficult."

Across the country we have the same values about what is a good society and a desirable political culture. We all recognize too, the benefits of an economic and monetary union. But sadly, just as we have come to agree as never before on fundamental values and to recognize our economic interdependence, we are closer to breakup than ever before. Our alternative visions of the nation are more forcefully articulated and seemingly more irreconcilable. Charles Taylor, in an essay in *Options for a New Canada,* has eloquently articulated and explored the dilemma, especially as it relates to tensions between Quebec and the rest of Canada.

He poses two questions: Why Canada and why Quebec? He identifies five distinctive features of Canada to explain the reasons for its existence. It has less violence and conflict, and more commitment to law and order than the United States; it is more committed to collective provision and help; it is committed to the equalization of the conditions of life and opportunity across the regions; it is committed to multiculturalism; it is committed to the *Canadian Charter of Rights and Freedoms*.

Quebec sees most of these as good, but they are not its starting point. Quebec sees itself as a nation and seeks more legislative powers to fashion itself. Quebec understands Canada as a pact between *"deux nations"* and the structure of the federation must follow from this.

To this divergence must be added the tensions between a centralized and decentralized federation and the emerging idea of self-governing, distinct aboriginal societies.

This divergence of national visions is greater than ever before, but we have a greater understanding of the nature and implications of them. Charles Taylor notes that accommodating differences is what Canada is all about and argues that we face a challenge to our very conception of diversity. "To build a country for everyone, Canada would have to allow for second-level or 'deep diversity', where a plurality of ways of belonging would also be acknowledged and accepted. Someone of, say, Italian extraction in Toronto, or of Ukrainian extraction in Edmonton, might indeed feel Canadian as a bearer of individual rights in a multicultural mosaic. His or her belonging would not 'pass through' some community, although the ethnic identity might be important to him or her in various ways. But this person might nevertheless accept that a Québécois, or a Cree, or a Déné, might belong in a different way, that they were Canadian through being members of their national communities. And reciprocally, the Québécois, Cree or Déné would accept the perfect legitimacy of the 'mosaic' identity."

If Canada is to remain together, each of the alternative visions must be compromised. No one vision can produce a stable consensus. Quebec cannot be so asymmetrically treated as to become a politically autonomous unit in the federation. Regional demands cannot be resolved by a drastically decentralized nation. Aboriginal peoples must remain citizens of both the aboriginal and Canadian nations. National concerns cannot be solely managed by the federal government, domineering over provincial activities. The *Canadian Charter of Rights and Freedoms* will have to be applied with exceptions.

Although we seem unable to resolve our divergent visions, splitting into separate countries is no solution. Most of the tensions will still remain in the new nations, particularly the need to accommodate aboriginal concerns. Such is the nature of pluralistic liberal societies. And as separate countries we would have to create supranational institutions to manage our interdependence.

There still remains a dangerous naiveté among many Canadians who believe that these divergences do not need to be addressed. Some say "Don't worry. Quebec won't go. We've been chattering away about the constitution for 125 years and we'll still be chattering on Canada's 150th birthday." This is quite wrong. The survival of Canada is truly at stake. Even were Quebec to remain, if the regional and aboriginal concerns are not dealt with, bitterness and rancour would permeate our national life for years to come.

Others say: "Let Quebec go. We'd both be better off." This is equally wrong. Both Quebec and Canada would suffer economically, and the rest of Canada would still be left with intractable constitutional problems. Disintegration or at least the dimming of Canada's distinctiveness under the American shadow are real possibilities.

If we are to amend our constitution and reconcile our divergent visions, there must be a process through which a compromise agreement is reached. At the end of the day, amendments can only be made by resolutions of the Senate, House of Commons and legislative assemblies of the provinces. There is no escape from this. The constitution specifies the amending formula. Some matters require unanimous consent, such as changes to the number of members a province sends to the House of Commons, the use of French and English, the composition of the Supreme Court and changes to the amending formula. Most other matters require consent of the Senate, House of Commons and the legislatures of at least two-thirds of the provinces that have at least 50 percent of the population.

The Meech Lake compromise was reached in private negotiations between the prime minister and ten premiers. Having reached an agreement, no amendment or alteration was allowed. The Accord was placed before the federal houses and the provincial legislatures, but did not receive unanimous consent, in part because the process itself was unacceptable to many Canadians.

In the aftermath of Meech, there was no generally accepted process for generating proposed amendments to the constitution. All manner of means were suggested by constitutional lawyers and academics. Some were wild and exotic and some were sensible. In retrospect, although at each stage it looked as if the process would collapse and no one knew what the next stage would be, we have done rather well. The Citizens' Forum on Canada's Future heard from hundreds of thousands of people and reported out. Provinces held constitutional hearings, Quebec produced the Allaire Report, the Group of 22 offered their model, and the federal government tabled proposals. Aboriginal peoples began a parallel process. Academics, constitutional experts, research institutes, journalists, interest groups and concerned individuals mulled over the reports and produced reactions and alternatives. A joint committee of the Senate and House of Commons toured the country hearing reaction to the federal proposals. Five constitutional conferences were held, bringing together interest groups, citizens and experts. The joint committee released the Beaudoin-Dobbie Report. It appeared as though the federal government wanted to draft the final proposals — with a tight deadline. But extensive negotiations were undertaken; the provinces and aboriginal peoples were included; Quebec sent observers; and the deadline was extended. More by good luck than good planning we are conducting a process. It has been open and all voices have been heard. We are still talking civilly to one another and no one has staked out a completely intransigent position. Amendments have been allowed and deadlines extended.

Perhaps most important of all, the fundamental issues have been isolated and explored. We have not resolved most of them: what we share and where we differ, the division of powers, the application of the Charter, the amending formula, the makeup of the Supreme Court, aboriginal self-government, the social charter, and so on. But the debate has been

Some Fundamental Questions to Consider

Economic Union
• Should the mobility of people, goods, services and capital be guaranteed?
• Should there be a common framework of business and social policies across the country?
• Should tax systems be similar across the country?
• Should federal and provincial fiscal policies be coordinated?

Monetary Union
• What should be the Bank of Canada's mandate?
• How should provinces and regions participate in shaping Bank policy?

Social Charter
• Should a social charter be in the constitution?
• What social programs should be included?
• Should a charter be binding on government decisions?
• Should we have a national sharing community or a series of linked provincial communities?

Federal Powers
• What powers should be exclusively federal? A minimal list might include: defence; international relations; currency and debt; equalization.
• Should the federal government have the primary responsibility for management of the economy?

Provincial Powers
• What powers should be exclusively provincial? A minimal list might include: education; health; natural resources; municipal affairs.
• Should provincial governments have the primary responsibility for social policy?
• What extra powers should Quebec have for its cultural and economic development?

Shared Powers
• What powers should be shared? A minimal list might include: agriculture; environment; immigration; language; culture.
• What should be the role of the federal spending power, which allows federal involvement in exclusively provincial areas?
• Should flexibility be achieved through concurrency, legislative delegation or intergovernmental agreements?

more open and complete than ever before. And although positions will no doubt harden as the time for a final decision arrives, we are in a much better position than seemed possible a year ago.

The economic dimensions of the Confederation debate have been given a great deal of attention. Economic analysis has identified three areas of inevitable interdependence; namely, the economic union, the monetary union and the social charter. Whatever constitutional structure we use, decentralized or asymmetric federalism or even two countries, these issues will have to be addressed. There is consensus on the need for and benefits from an economic and monetary union, although less so on the social charter. But a charter may be required for a balanced package and it does complete the social contract between citizen and state. The division of powers sets out the domain of government and assigns it to levels, the *Charter of Rights and Freedoms* places limits on governments, and the social charter would place obligations on government. We want our economy to produce both private goods and public services. A social charter sets out certain public services for special attention. It is noteworthy that European integration includes the same three elements: economic union, monetary union and a social charter. (And eventually it will include a form of political union.)

Economics provides a framework for the analysis of the division of powers. In a large, diverse country, the provision of public services should be decentralized to match the diversity of tastes. However, some government activities benefit the nation and should be a central responsibility. Economies of scale and externalities also increase the role for the central government. Much of what government does involves a redistribution from one group to another — from rich to poor, employed to unemployed, healthy to sick, wealthier province to poorer province and so on. If we wish a national sharing community, there will be a federal role in these redistributive activities. If we wish sharing to occur only within provinces, there will not. Preserving mobility within the economic union will require coordination and a degree of harmonization of social policy across the country. Taxing powers may be assigned to match expenditure responsibilities, but economies of scale, the need for national economic management and for harmonized tax structures in an economic union can mean taxing and expenditure powers diverge. Balance is restored through intergovernmental transfers. Examination of powers on a case-by-case basis using the economics framework reveals they cannot be placed in watertight compartments and divided unambiguously among levels of government. There is inevitable overlap of powers and interdependence of levels.

Ultimately, the choice of federal structures depends upon the difference in organizational costs, comprehensively defined, of running the government institutions for carrying out a policy. None of the constitutional proposals has carefully examined these organizational costs.

Canada is faced with severe economic challenges. We have a fiscal crisis and over the medium term must return government deficits and debt to manageable levels. We must increase innovation and productivity in a world of increasing economic integration and competition. We must improve our ability to control inflation without requiring a punishing level of unemployment. We must sustain an economy and system of government that can provide the social programs desired by Canadians. The final conclusions of the economics of the confederation debate are several and simple.

• We cannot meet our pressing economic challenges without a resolution of our constitutional dilemma.

• The separation of Quebec from Canada would leave everyone worse off, at least in the short and medium term. This is as true for the rest of Canada as for Quebec.

• Our future prosperity requires that we at least maintain our current level of economic integration.

• Economic integration cannot be sustained without some form of political integration. Small units must cede sovereignty either to supranational institutions or to a national government.

BIBLIOGRAPHY

Constitutional Background

Banting, Keith G. and Richard Simeon, eds. *Redesigning the State: The Politics of Constitutional Change in Industrial Countries.* Toronto: University of Toronto Press, 1986.

Business Council on National Issues. *A Citizen's Guide to the Constitutional Question.* Toronto: Gage Publishing Limited, 1980.

Canada. Citizens' Forum on Canada's Future. *Citizens' Forum on Canada's Future: Report to the People and Government of Canada* [The Spicer Report]. Ottawa: Supply and Services, 1991.

Canada. Department of Justice. *The Constitution Acts, 1867 to 1982.* Ottawa: Queen's Printer, 1989.

Alternative Constitutional Structures

Bercuson, David J. and Barry Cooper. *Deconfederation: Canada Without Quebec.* Toronto: Key Porter Books, 1991.

Canada. Minister of Supply and Services. *Shaping Canada's Future Together: Proposals.* Ottawa: Supply and Services, 1991.

Canada. Special Joint Committee. *Report of the Special Joint Committee on a Renewed Canada* [Beaudoin-Dobbie Report]. Ottawa: Queen's Printer, 1992.

The Group of 22. *Some Practical Suggestions for Canada: Report of the Group of 22.* June 1991.

Liberal Party of Quebec. *A Québec Free to Choose* [The Allaire Report]. Quebec City: 1991.

Ontario. Ministry of Intergovernmental Affairs. *A Canadian So-*

cial Charter: Making Our Shared Values Stronger. Toronto: Intergovernmental Affairs, 1991.

Watts, Ronald L. and Douglas M. Brown, eds. *Options for a New Canada.* Toronto: University of Toronto Press, 1991.

Economics of Constitutional Reform

The Macdonald Commission

Canada. Minister of Supply and Services. *Report of the Royal Commission on the Economic Union and Development Prospects for Canada.* Vol. 59 *Federalism and Economic Union in Canada.* Vol. 60 *Perspectives on the Canadian Economic Union.* Vol. 68 *Regional Aspects of Confederation.* Ottawa: Supply and Services, 1985.

John Deutsch Institute Series

Boadway, Robin W., Thomas J. Courchene, and Douglas D. Purvis, eds. *Economic Dimensions of Constitutional Change,* 2 vols. Kingston: Queen's University, 1991.

Boadway, Robin W. and Douglas D. Purvis, eds. *Economic Aspects of the Federal Government's Constitutional Proposals.* Kingston: Queen's University, 1991.

C.D. Howe Institute Canada Round Series

Courchene, Thomas J. *In Praise of Renewed Federalism.* Toronto: C.D. Howe Institute, 1991.

Laidler, David E. W. *How Shall We Govern the Governor? A Critique of the Governance of the Bank of Canada.* Toronto: C.D. Howe Institute, 1991.

Laidler, David E.W. and William B.P. Robson. *Two Nations, One Money? Canada's Monetary System Following a Quebec Secession.* Toronto: C.D. Howe Institute, 1991.

McCallum, John and Chris Green. *Parting as Friends: The Economic Consequences for Quebec*. Toronto: C.D. Howe Institute, 1991.

Ritchie, Gordon, Ronald J. Wonnacott, W.H. Furton, R.S. Gray, Richard G. Lipsey, and Rodrique Tremblay. *Broken Links: Trade Relations after a Quebec Secession*. Toronto: C.D. Howe Institute, 1991.

Other Studies

Breton, Albert. *Centralization, Decentralization and Intergovernmental Competition*. Kenneth R. MacGregor Lecture. Kingston: Institute for Intergovernmental Affairs, Queen's University, 1989.

Canada. Minister of Supply and Services. *Canadian Federalism and the Economic Union: Partnership for Prosperity*. Ottawa: Supply and Services, 1991.

————. *The European Community: A Political Model for Canada?* Ottawa: Supply and Services, 1991.

————. *A Joint Venture: The Economics of Constitutional Options*. Twenty-Eighth Annual Review of the Economic Council of Canada.

————. *Transitions for the 90s*. Twenty-Seventh Annual Review of the Economic Council of Canada.

Grady, Patrick. *The Economic Consequences of Quebec Sovereignty*. Vancouver: The Fraser Institute, 1991.

Western Centre for Economic Research. *Alberta and the Economics of Constitutional Change*. Alberta: University of Alberta, 1991.

The National Finances

Canada. The Department of Finance. *The Budget*. February 20, 1990. Ottawa: Department of Finance, 1990.

——. *The Budget*. February 26, 1991. Ottawa: Department of Finance, 1991.

——. *The Budget*. February 25, 1992. Ottawa: Department of Finance, 1992.

——. *Quarterly Economic Review*. June 1991. Ottawa: Queen's Printer, 1991.

Canada. Minister of Industry, Science and Technology. *Provincial Economic Accounts* (Statistics Canada 13-210). Annual.

Canada. Minister of Supply and Services. *Income After Tax, Distribution by Size in Canada*. Annual.

Ip, Irene K. *Big Spenders: A Survey of Provincial Government Finances in Canada*. Toronto: C.D. Howe Institute, 1991.

McMillan, Melville, ed. *Provincial Public Finances*, 2 vols. Toronto: Canadian Tax Foundation, 1991.

The National Finances. Toronto: Canadian Tax Foundation, 1990.

OECD. *OECD Economic Outlook*. 49 (July 1991).